Beams Falling:
The Art of Dashiell Hammett

Beams Falling:
The Art of Dashiell Hammett

Peter Wolfe

Bowling Green University Popular Press
Bowling Green, Ohio 43403

ISBN: 0-87972-139-1 CB
ISBN: 0-87972-140-5 PB

To

Mary Geere of Worthing

May she flourish

Cover design by Vicki Heninger

Acknowledgments

The author and publisher join in expressing their thanks to those whose time and energy went into the preparation of this book: Theresa Orso, who typed the manuscript; William F. Nolan, who both supplied important insights into Hammett and read the typescript; Francis M. Nevins, Jr., who helped give the book its first push by furnishing me out-of-print material by Hammett, then discussed the typescript with me, and even gave me the book's title. I can say safely that the help Mr. Nevins gave me was indispensable; without it I would have written a weaker book with a less apt title.

The combined help of the following people amounts to a major contribution: Sande Kalmar, William A. Clarke, Mickey Jean Jade, George Filancia, Sindy Lai, James Roark, Lionel Harding, May Blog, Edwin Coates, and Donald Voet.

CONTENTS

1

The Detective Nobody Knew

Dashiell Hammett is nothing at all if he isn't mysterious. Although dead less than twenty years, he left so little of himself behind that he has already become an enigma—and a problem. His ex-biographer, Steven Marcus, refers to "Hammett's extraordinary carelessness, his apparent lack of interest in preserving the record of his existence."[1] Because of this sparseness, Marcus had to hire a detective to plug the gaps. Did the detective turn up much material? Perhaps less than we might reasonably hope: Lillian Hellman, Hammett's close friend for many years, says that the dearth of information surviving Hammett comes less from neglect than from design. She argues well. The little that Hammett left to posterity makes him look like a man who covered his tracks. And covered them carefully: the more personal the detail, the less he told about it. The man who wrote better about liars, hypocrites, and prevaricators than any American novelist since Henry James knew the concealment operation root and branch. People who either knew him or have written about him refer to his passion for privacy. Ralph Harper, in *The World of the Thriller* (1969), calls him one of those writers "unwilling to share with anyone all they know of themselves"[2] The title character of Joe Gores's 1975 novel, *Hammett,* set in San Francisco in 1928, hasn't told his sweetheart about his estranged wife and two daughters. The real-life Hammett also held back from his female friends. Lillian Hellman knew him well enough to avoid asking him why he stopped writing fiction after *The Thin Man* (1934). "He was a man," she says in the short biographical headnote to the omnibus edition of his novels, *The Novels of Dashiell Hammett* (1965), "who kept his work, and his plans for work, in angry privacy." His work wasn't the only part of his life he kept private. He wouldn't talk either about his Marxism or the illness that wore him down and finally broke him: "Dash would always make fun of trouble or pain; that was one way he could handle it,"[3] said Miss Hellman five years after his death. Privacy and evasion claimed more and more of him. He spent the years 1952-56 in a small, out-of-the-way cottage in Katonah, New York, his mail unanswered, and both his typewriter and phonograph, symbols of communication with the outside world, neglected.[4] His last years, which he spent in New York City, were just as reclusive. Finally, the refusal to face himself halted his writing career.

The skimpiness of biographical data about Hammett has caused some strange reverberations. Writing in the special Hammett number of the *City of San Francisco* magazine (4 November 1975), Marcus tells us that Hammett lived and worked in many places—Baltimore, San Francisco, New York, Hollywood, and the Aleutians—and that all of them claim him as a son.[5] Another article in the same issue by Joe Gores pinpoints various San Francisco hotels, office buildings, apartments, and restaurants that figure in the Hammett canon. "A brass plaque today marks the spot of [Miles] Archer's demise"[6] near Burritt Street, Gores says in his section of *The Maltese Falcon*. Nor is Gores's the only recent magazine article written in the spirit of the Baker Street Irregulars. Fritz Leiber's "Stalking Sam Spade," which appeared in the Sunday supplement, *California Living*, of the 13 January 1974 issue of the San Francisco *Examiner and Chronicle*, also treats the characters of *The Maltese Falcon* as actual people, searching out the real-life originals of settings in the book with a nice blend of nostalgia, fun, and objectivity.

Most of what is known of Hammett's sparsely documented life can be found in William F. Nolan's pioneering book, *Dashiell Hammett: A Casebook* (1969). Samuel Dashiell Hammett was born 27 May 1894 in St. Mary's County, Maryland. His father's ancestry was Scots; that of his mother, *née* De Chiel (later Englished to Dashiell), was French. Raised a Roman Catholic in Baltimore and Philadelphia, Hammett

2

left school at age thirteen to work as a newsboy, messenger, freight clerk, timekeeper, stevedore, and yardman. At the age of twenty or so, he began working as an operative for the Pinkerton Detective Agency, a job he held till June 1918, when he enlisted in the U.S. Army. Military life brought both rewards and setbacks. Though he rose to the rank of sergeant in the Motor Ambulance Corps, he found himself posted only twenty miles from already familiar Baltimore. He also contracted tuberculosis while in uniform and had to spend two years in army hospitals in Tacoma and San Diego getting his lungs repaired. In Tacoma, he met Josephine Anna Dolan, an army nurse he was to marry in 1921. The couple moved to San Francisco, where they had two daughters and then lived apart before breaking for good some time around 1930 *(Maltese Falcon* [1930] is dedicated to her). To support himself and his family, he rejoined the Pinkertons for a colorful eight-month hitch, testifying in the notorious Fatty Arbuckle rape case.

After giving up detective work, he wrote advertising copy for the San Francisco jeweller Albert B. Samuels, to whom he dedicated his second novel, *The Dain Curse,* in 1929. He left Samuels this same year to write fiction full time; since 1922, he had been publishing short stories, mostly in *Black Mask,* the first pulp magazine to feature the gunplay, tough cynicism, and lean vernacular prose known today as hardboiled. Hammett worked hard at his writing for the five years after leaving Samuels, publishing short stories and all five of his novels. Then he migrated between Hollywood and New York, writing radio plays, film scripts, and, with the cartoonist Alexander Raymond, the syndicated comic strip, *Secret Agent X-9,* for King Features. Big contracts rolled in, Lillian Hellman calling him "the hottest thing in Hollywood and New York"[7] during the 1930s. A great deal of the money generated by this heat went quickly on gambling and drink. But cash kept coming, if not from writing or book sales, then from films based on *The Maltese Falcon* (three between 1931-41) or *The Thin Man* (five between 1934-44).

The shock waves sent through the country by Pearl Harbor also rocked Hammett. Ironically, the man later jailed for subversiveness enlisted in the U.S. Signal Corps in 1942, at age forty-eight. After training at Fort Monmouth, New Jersey, he served in the Aleutians, where he edited a daily newspaper. Before his discharge as a sergeant in 1945, at age fifty-one, he saw duty in Anchorage and Edmonton, Alberta. Civilian life brought little to thaw the northern cold.

3

Continued hard drinking both weakened his constitution for a bout against emphysema and sapped his creativity. Though he taught writing at New York's Jefferson School of Social Science, he never finished the play or the novel he had started after the war. Royalties on paperback reprints of his work supported his drinking, which he finally stopped on doctor's orders. But trouble continued to stalk him. His left-wing political activity in the 1930s brought him before a Congressional committee, costing him a five-month jail term in 1951. This ordeal shattered a constitution already marred by years of fast living. His last ten years saw Hammett a frail, haggard man. In January 1961, at the age of sixty-six, he died of inoperable lung cancer.

This eminently gifted, fiercely private man had a short writing career, publishing over sixty stories and five novels between 1922-34. Why he stopped writing at age forty will never be known. Several explanations have been given. But to cite restlessness, intellectual fatigue, or Hollywood, with its promise of easy money and easy women, is to neglect the steeliness of Hammett's mind. Hammett wrote about what he did or what he knew. His having had the good sense to stick to the fresh and the first-hand helped him give American detective writing a strength it had never known before. This new realism, more than anything else, has won him acceptance as both America's most important detective writer since Poe and the father of the hardboiled mystery story. By 1934, he had acquired professional polish to go along with his skills as a natural storyteller. But he had also run out of material. Rather than writing about what he was, i.e., himself, he stopped writing. Ironically, his silence came at a time when, like so many other artists, he might have enjoyed the creative bursts of early maturity. But artists don't always live by the calendar. The same need for privacy that sealed his lips before the House Un-American Activities Committee in 1951, when speaking out could have kept him out of jail without incriminating anybody, turned him from fiction-writing in 1934. He would write about his experiences, but not about how they touched his heart. His feelings he kept to himself, but at the cost of relegating his works to the ranks of minor fiction. Major literature, always a combined self-exploration and self-discovery, conveys the author's feelings both about himself and his environment. Hammett didn't test himself deeply enough to give his work this finality and scope. Moral vision *qua* psychological thrust exists but marginally in the canon.

4

But Hammett wasn't a moral quietist. He simply chose a different medium with which to share his moral conscience with others, increasingly searching out political, rather than personal, solutions to human problems. He was wooed by Marxism in the 1920s or 1930s; in 1942, he became president of the Writers' League of America; he joined the Army the same year; then he headed the New York branch of the Civil Rights Congress. Sadly, this *bon vivant* and political activist ended his days a near-hermit.

This incongruity is but one of many in Hammett's life. His greatest period of artistic activity, achievement, and recognition, 1929-34, coincided with the nation's deepest economic woes. He wrote *The Thin Man,* a novel set mostly in an elegant suite of an expensive New York hotel, while living in a Times Square fleabag just blocks away. Once, he hired a chauffeured limousine to repay a debt that fell far short of the limousine hire. Though a Marxist, he threw money around during the Depression without wasting a scruple on the suffering of the proletariat. This rift between conviction and practice suggests that his explanation of his drinking problem in the autobiographical fragment, *Tulip,* rests on a failing that applies as strictly to him as to others: "I drank a lot in those days, partly because I was still confused by the fact that people's feelings and talk and actions didn't have much to do with one another." But the sharpest incongruity comes in his turning away from the novel, with its built-in endorsement of individuality, in favor of politics. Did he lose faith in man's ability both to know and to save himself individually? *The Thin Man* interpolates a story of the Mountain West, "Alfred Packer, 'The Maneater,' " whose cannibalism implies that the dismemberment of the social body leads to the killing and dismemberment of the person.

But Hammett had questioned his novelistic stance well before his last book. Marcus has compared the goals and methods of the detective with those of the novelist. In his introduction to the 1974 collection of stories, *The Continental Op,* Marcus speaks of "a reflexive and coordinate relation between the activities of the Op [the stories' detective-narrator] and the activities of the writer . . . The work of the detective is a fiction-making activity, a discovery or fabrication of something new . . . or undeveloped."[8] The comparison is well judged: both novelist and detective respect probability, study motives, and use empirical evidence to discover both causes and meanings. In Hammett's case, the comparison pushes into the realm of the psyche.

5

Hammett, let us remember, gave up both detection and fiction after about the same amount of time; though his twelve-year literary career bested his tenure as a sleuth by four years, he only wrote full time from 1929-33; furthermore, his Army service and subsequent illness meant that, over an eight-year period starting in 1914, he only worked two and a half years as a detective. Nolan's remarks on the finale of *The Dain Curse,* where the killer turns out to be a novelist, hints revealingly at Hammett's dissatisfaction with both trades: "This is Hammett having his joke: the novelist naming a novelist as a mad villain. . . . His portrait of Fitzstephan might well have served as a self-description."9

Nolan's witty comparison can be extended. Few mystery stories support the traditional claim that the crime writer splits his psyche between lawman and outlaw more forcibly than *The Dain Curse.* Both the Continental Op (so called because he works as an operative for the Continental Detective Agency) and Owen Fitzstephan move from the east to the west coast. The two men also spend time together and stake a common territory in both places. Whereas Fitzstephan commits the crimes Op investigates in San Francisco, he was "plowing the same field for literary material" in New York that Op was plowing to find an extortionist. Throughout, the men act as halves of a single personality—one committing crimes, the other investigating them; one yielding to the lure of sex, the other resisting; one indulging the fantastic and the grotesque, his counterpart acting from motives of common sense and good will. Sometimes, the men take turns interpreting the action. In Chapter 3, Hammett links them rhetorically. Just after trading accusations of spying, they respond to each other with the same phrasing and the same sentence rhythms:

"Are you—who make your living snooping—sneering at my curiosity . . .?"

"We're different," I said. "I do mine with the object of putting people in jail, and I get paid for it, though not as much as I should."

"That's not different," he said. "I do mine with the object of putting people in books, and I get paid for it, though not as much as I should."

Crime fighting and crime fiction must remain distinct, any attempt to wrench the parallel between them inducing disorder and pain. Ambition brings Fitzstephan to grief. He must carry his artistry into life, founding and organizing the religious cult that does so much mischief in the middle sections of the novel. But the destructive interplay be-

6

tween the real and the imagined flows reversibly. The Op's metaphor describing his fight with an apparition concocted by the cult, "The ghost had me sweating ink," shows the actionist encroaching, if only figuratively, upon the realm of the writer in a time of hardship.

Elsewhere in the canon, artistic activity fuses with shame and death. For a while, it seems that the murder victim in "The Tenth Clew" (1924) was bludgeoned to death by a typewriter. "Nightmare Town" (1927) deepens the implication. The story's archcriminal is a man named Rymer, who practices the art, not of rhyming, or poetry, but of feigning blindness; for months, he has tricked all his neighbors into believing him blind. A physical feature of Rymer mentioned at least twice is the "paperish" skin on his neck. Now paper is a dead skin, a flat, thin, dry membrane yielding no leaves or fruit. That it is also the substance on which stories are both written and printed reinstates Hammett's disdain of fiction-writing. That the villain's name, Rymer, invokes poetry slants this disdain toward fiction that is intimate, sudden, and rhythmical. Hammett's practice of describing surface action rather than sounding psychological depths again comes to the fore. The more revealing a story, i.e., the closer a story resembles a poem, the greater his uneasiness.

Sometimes the uneasiness is treated lightly. "Second-Story Angel" (1923) shows four crime writers fooled by the same young woman playing the same trick. Angel Grace burgles the apartment of each writer with studied ineptitude at a time she is sure to be caught. Each writer, seeing her as a rich source of narrative materials, gives the policeman about to arrest her several hundred dollars to turn a blind eye. Each arranges to meet her the next day. Each is stood up. The burglaries and subsequent arrests had both been staged, the arresting policeman leaguing with, rather than contending against, the pretty young thief. Having planned their operation beforehand, the two accomplices chose a name for the thief, Angel Grace, whose pointed symbolism would disarm a literary man. They chose well. Hammett's artists and intellectuals are almost always defeated by some such maneuver. Robin Thin, the poet-sleuth of "The Nails in Mr. Cayterer" (1926) and the posthumously published "A Man Named Thin" (1962), gets by unbruised, but he is the detective-narrator in both stories. Others dedicated to the mind or the imagination meet worse ends, like Dudley Morey, the weakling artist of "The Joke on Eloise Morey" (1923), whose vicious wife drives him to suicide. Two

7

characters Hammett identifies with, because of their tuberculosis, are Dan Rolff of *Red Harvest* (1929) and Ned Beaumont of *The Glass Key* (1931). Both are victims. The truthsaying Rolff is shamed by the woman he loves before getting beaten up and killed. If his wisdom is ineffectual, that of Beaumont causes harm—mostly to himself. Beaumont's close tie to a city boss leads to several terrific poundings by the boss's rival when Beaumont refuses to divulge information. His illness, his gambling, his sensitivity, and his pride all link him to Hammett. The poundings he gets link him to a modern cultural tradition. The idea of the physical suffering of the artist (here, his stand-in) goes back to Schopenhauer, Freud, and Joyce, all of whom saw the artist as a misfit whose neurotic unfitness for the everyday world forces him to fabricate his own. This other world has *its* place on the century's cultural map; for the suffering of Hammett's artists and intellectuals also meshes with Marxist polemic. Marxism's strong activist bias downgrades intellectualism as sterile and empty; we learn about life through direct participation, not through reading and writing, says communist writ.

But how does the writ apply to Hammett? Like so much else about him, his communism remains a puzzle. Lillian Hellman never knew whether he was a party member at all. Rarely did he act like one during his writing heyday. But did he need to? If he hadn't joined the party or at least bought its doctrine, he did remember breaking workers' strikes as a Pinkerton. Stories like "Eloise Morey" and "Second-Story Angel" reflect a Marxist contempt for all (including artists) not furthering the class war and the workers' revolution. Even though this contempt may not have been Marxist inspired, it carried smoothly into any number of Marxist social programs that won popularity in the 1930s. His disenchantment with writing makes it reasonable to assume that Hammett's failure to yoke detective fiction to Marxism, as G.K. Chesterton yoked it to Roman Catholicism in the Father Brown stories, finished him as a writer. Hammett would only accept things on his own harsh terms. His lonely pride made him prefer prison to freedom in 1951, when freedom meant violating his private concept of democracy. Analogously, Sam Spade's pride keeps him from telling his questioners that he knows nothing about the Maltese falcon. And Ned Beaumont searches out his former assailants, thus inviting another beating, rather than showing them his fears; honor counts more than the flesh. But it isn't always satisfied by a stroke of will.

The job of resolving the alien requirements of Marx and literary detection could well defeat a person whose implacable honor ruled out compromise. It could even make him gamble and drink.

I

The works Hammett didn't write must give way to the ones he did. To move from surmising about what never happened in favor of discussing the real and the achieved is to clear a path to the art of fast-paced adventure and intrigue. Hammett has the craft of good narration well in hand. He writes fresh, muscular prose; he controls his materials; he knows how to seize and then hold the reader. The vigor, rhythm, and discreet detailing of its opening paragraph, for instance, get "The Gutting of Couffignal" (1925) off to a fast start:

> Wedge-shaped Couffignal is not a large island, and not far from the mainland, to which it is linked by a wooden bridge. Its western shore is a high, straight cliff that jumps abruptly up out of San Pablo Bay. From the top of this cliff the island slopes eastward, down to a smooth pebble beach that runs into the water again, where there are piers and a clubhouse and moored pleasure boats.

Much of Hammett's best work sustains this vibrancy by means of color, concreteness, and a sharp eye for both social detail and historical change. Sometimes, he wins the day by avoiding vibrancy. The precision of flat, bald factual statements recounted in toneless sequence conveys menace in the 1929 story, "Fly Paper"; "Babe liked Sue. Vassos liked Sue. Sue liked Babe. Vassos didn't like that." "The Scorched Face" (1925) evokes horror in its picture of a corpse. But rather than showing the horror, it uses indirect statement. Hammett doesn't say what some birds have done to disfigure a girl's corpse; he doesn't need to. Having been roused to activity, our imaginations complete the grisly picture: "At the base of a tree, on her side, her knees drawn up close to her body, a girl was dead. She wasn't nice to see. Birds had been at her."

Most often, Hammett stirs our imaginations by using forms and norms traditionally associated with crime fiction. He knew the aesthetic limits of his medium and kept within them. The detective novels he reviewed for the *Saturday Review of Literature* between 1927-29 and the techniques reflected in his own work both show his familiarity with the formal conventions of mysteries. The long set piece joining an unsolved crime to its roots in the past, from Conan Doyle's *Study in Scarlet, The Sign of Four,* and *The Valley of Fear,* appears in Edgar Leggett's (Maurice Pierre de Mayenne's) letter about his European and Latin American ordeals in *The Dain Curse.* The dream sequences in *Red Harvest* and *The Glass Key,* the cannibalism in *The Thin Man,* and the suburban businessman Charles Flitcraft's roundabout move from Spokane to Tacoma in *The Maltese Falcon* create a link more imaginative than historical. The role of the narrator's review of Arthur Edward Waite's *The Brotherhood of the Holy Cross* in *Tulip,* written some twenty-five years before the time of the unfinished novel, can't be known. But its very appearance in a book which has nothing to do with detection conveys Hammett's ongoing practice of mining classic detective fiction for plotting devices.

Conan Doyle isn't his only source. Sometimes, he uses devices popular among his contemporaries. As in Ellery Queen's *Roman Hat Mystery* (1929), the first three corpses of "House Dick" materialize under bizarre circumstances when three dead bodies tumble out of a closet, falling on top of each other. This 1923 story, like "Nightmare Town" and *Red Harvest* after it, uses a device familiar to much of Ellery Queen—the dying message. Hammett's growing skill with the device shows clearly in a comparison between its use in "When Luck's Running Good" (1923) and *Red Harvest.* The dying man's unfinished identification in *Red Harvest* supplies a suspect and a set of motives that power the action till it needs redirecting. Here is the Op's explanation for misinterpreting the message: "He [the dying man] didn't say *Whisper.* I've heard women call Thaler *Max,* but I've never heard a man here call him anything but Whisper. Tim didn't say *Max.* He said MacS—the first part of *MacSwain*—and died before he could finish it." The crafting of the dying message in "When Luck's Running Good" is clumsy, by comparison, Near the end of the story, the villain resolves the action for Hammett by killing himself and leaving a suicide note. His dying message is written, to prevent misunderstanding; furthermore, it is written in English so we can discover its contents together with the characters who read it, even though its writer is a Russian exile new to the United States.

If the dying message can resolve or complicate an action, the chase can be counted on to keep one hot and lively. Hammett's ability to make the chase motif achieve different thematic goals reveals him a master of melodrama. Pursuit can speed the formation of, and even create, a personal tie. "Woman in the Dark" (1933) shows two strangers on the run, forced together by a common danger stemming from a common enemy. The urgency of their purpose forms a bond between the man and the woman it would have taken Hammett pages to develop otherwise. Chases vary in style and complexity. In "The Gatewood Caper" (1923), the first story Hammett published (as "Crooked Souls") under his own name, a kidnapper wears women's clothing to pick up his ransom payment and then ducks into a dark alley to shed his disguise. "Fly Paper," a deft blend of mind and muscle by the Op, contains an auto chase which sustains buoyancy and snap till the manhunt carries forward on foot. In "This King Business" (1928), where the Op is shadowed at the same time he's shadowing someone else, the piggyback chase pattern looks ahead to those in Graham Greene's *This Gun for Hire* (1936) and Frederick Forsyth's *The Day of the Jackal* (1971). This pursuit, like most of the others in Hammett, takes place in the dark, evoking fear, confusion, and malignancy. In contrast to the sunlit English country house mystery, where evil is isolated, the American hardboiled story underscores the vision of widescale corruption it puts forth by setting many of its main actions at night—the shootout in which Philip Marlowe kills his captor in Raymond Chandler's *The Big Sleep* (1939); Spillane's first chapter of *Kiss Me, Deadly* (1952), where Mike Hammer's car burns and his hitchhiker gets murdered; the finale of Ross Macdonald's *The Chill* (1964), which shows a woman ramming her car into that of her much-younger husband. Hammett follows the standard practice. Fights occur in the dark in "It" (1923), "The House on Turk Street" (1924), "The Girl with the Silver Eyes" (1924), "The Whosis Kid" (1925), and "Dead Yellow Women" (1925). "The Gutting of Couffignal" describes an island resort both without electricity and under siege in the dark. Donald Willsson, the Op's client, gets shot to death on a dark, lonely street in *Red Harvest,* as do murder victims in "Death on Pine Street" (1924) and *The Glass Key* (1931). The title character of "Who Killed Bob Teal" (1924) dies on a dark, empty lot. Finally, the bullets that kill Donald Willsson and Sam Spade's partner, Miles Archer, are fired from dark alleys. In both deaths, the sharpness of Hammett's prose and his accuracy of observation

11

impart realism to the melodrama, giving it an authority beyond that of most *Black Mask* fiction.

Noting a change rather than a development in Hammett, John G. Cawelti see this authority infusing a spectrum of literary conventions and modes:

> Hammett's early stories grew directly out of the pulp tradition and many of them, like *Red Harvest,* resemble westerns as much as they do detective stories . . . *The Dain Curse* makes use of a wide variety of gothic traditions . . . while *The Maltese Falcon* reflects the great tradition of stories of hidden treasure like "The Gold-Bug." . . . *The Thin Man* embodies a more contemporaneous literary tradition, the novel of high society and urban sophistication.[10]

Hammett's treatment of guilt reveals the creativity of his borrowing. In "$106,000 Blood Money" (1927), the gangland czar the Op wants to catch and arrest is known from the start. But one of his lieutenants turns out to be a colleague at the Continental Detective Agency. This work is only one of several in which the culprit and the sleuth have a bond. As has been seen, the villain is an old friend of the Op in *The Dain Curse*. The murderer in *Falcon* is the detective's lover; in *Thin Man,* it is an ex-army mate of the detective; and in Hammett's last *Black Mask* story and last in the Op series, "Death and Company" (November 1930), the client is the killer. Like guilt, time follows no predictable curve in the canon. A story of continuous action, "Couffignal" takes place in the time it takes the narrator to tell it. "The Whosis Kid," a story of about the same length, covers seven or eight years. In addition, its geographical borders extend from Boston to San Francisco, whereas those of "The House on Turk Street" a work that observes the unities of time and setting even more strictly than "Couffignal," stay within a one-story San Francisco home.

Hammett's fiction includes technical similarities as well as differences. For instance, recurring plot devices and character types animate the work. The spoiled headstrong daughter of a rich father appears in "The Gatewood Caper," "The Scorched Face," "$106,000 Blood Money," "Fly Paper," and *The Glass Key.* Adultery occurs in "The Barber and His Wife" (1922), "In the Morgue" (1922), "Eloise Morey," "Death on Pine Street," "The Scorched Face," "The Main Death" (1927), *The Dain Curse, Falcon,*

12

and *Thin Man;* the title of Hammett's 1924 story, "Zigzags of Treachery," refers to a tangle of betrayals which includes sex. Sexual enticement or temptation as a means of lowering a man's guard is a specialty of Hammett's women, getting into several Op stories, like "Silver Eyes," "The Whosis Kid," "Couffignal," *Red Harvest,* and *The Dain Curse,* the Sam Spade classic, *Falcon,* and the little-known story of the Mountain West, "The Man Who Killed Dan Odams" (1924). This highly accomplished work shows Dan Odams's killer escaping a Jingo, Montana jail, crossing some rough, wintry landscape, and having his horse shot from under him before finding food and shelter at the shack of a small, quiet woman. As soon as he explains his recent trials, he notices his nondescript hostess blossoming into alluring womanhood: "She bent to pick up a sack from the floor," he notices, observing further, "Under the thin pink dress the line of back and hips and legs stood out sharply against the wall." This shadow-game of sexual provocation edges into guile when, on the next page, the yet-unnamed woman leaves the shack housing the fugitive three times. Sustaining and developing the symbolism, several bullets fired from the rear door of the shack rip into the fugitive at the very moment he is pulling on the trousers of the woman's absent husband. The naming of the woman, Mrs. Odams, a page from the end, shows how far Hammett has taken us and how smoothly he has gotten us there. Few stories have such inevitability; few use details more convincingly, yet more subtly, to point their endings. Given what has happened and where, the story had to end as it did, down to its violent climax, where the fugitive gets shot putting on the pants of his murder victim because a trailing pant-leg trips him and foils his aim.

"Dan Odams" isn't Hammett's only story of the frontier. "Nightmare Town" (1927) takes place in the wild desert town of Izzard. Vultures, coyotes, and cowhands "hell bent on proving to everybody that they're just as tough as everybody else" bring Corkscrew, Arizona to gritty life in "Corkscrew," a 1925 Op story that predates by four years *Red Harvest,* which is usually regarded as the first of many works belonging to the "rotten town" genre. Hammett will sometimes take the Op out of San Francisco, his swift, sophisticated mind encompassing characters and settings remote from the dark urbanism of most hardboiled fiction. Besides the westerns, he also wrote "This King Business," a tale of intrigue, where new world energy and money cut across Balkan politics in the manner of

13

Anthony Hope's *Prisoner of Zenda* (1894). Other foreign settings flesh out the Hammett landscape. Hammett's first story to see print in *Black Mask* "The Road Home" (1922), takes place along a jungle river in Burma. The riddle posed by its finale takes on a shudder from the Conradian quiet—created by the foreign word, the slow, winding sentence rhythms, and the voiceless consonants—of the last paragraph:

> For five hours the captain kept the *jahaz* at anchor, and then, when the shadows of the trees on the west bank were creeping out into the river, he ordered the latten sail hoisted, and the teak craft vanished around the bend in the river.

Hammett wrote about the southwest Pacific at least once more. Set in the Sulu Archipelago, near Borneo, "Ber-Bulu" (1925), reprinted as "The Hairy One" by Ellery Queen in 1947, pits Moro simplicity against Christian wile. Hammett's extraordinary description of the story's brutish six-foot-six, three-hundred-pound main character—voiced by an effete gentleman-adventurer—looks ahead to other notable grotesques in the canon, like Casper Gutman of *Falcon*. Ross Macdonald thought enough of "Ber-Bulu" to include it as one of two works discussed in his 1964 mini-essay, for the *Mystery Writers' Annual,* "Homage to Dashiell Hammett," the other being *Falcon.* The admirable contrast between the passion described and the passionless narrator reveals Hammett a smooth technician as well as an adroit cultural comparativist. Hopefully, the story will be reprinted soon, giving a new generation of readers the chance to see Hammett display narrative skills usually not credited to him.

Hammett's economy of means lends his foreign settings both physical and imaginative presence. The perimeters of "The Golden Horseshoe" (1924) extend from Seattle to Tijuana, where about half the action takes place. Egypt, China, and France serve as red herrings, misdirecting our attention from the culprits, who stand in open view in "The Tenth Clew" (1924), "The Nails in Mr. Cayterer" (1926), and "The Farewell Murder" (1930). In *Falcon,* the *Paloma* sails to San Francisco from Hong Kong, smudging a character's nose with an ash from its burning hull and introducing a copy of the treasured bird many have died trying to possess. While *Paloma* smolders in San Francisco harbor, greed burns in the hearts of those contending for its deathly cargo. In "The Big Knockover" (1927), as well, evil invades the city as crooks from all over the country flood San Francisco to rob two large banks. *Red Harvest* varies the pattern. Here, municipal corruption begins when strike-breakers brought to town by the local mine owner decide to stay in Personville. But also coming to Personville, just as he had come to Corkscrew, Arizona, is the Op, representing the law. Greed hasn't engulfed all.

The Op's usual beat, San Francisco, with its harbor and international population, has a harder time shutting out crime than the desert. Combining the exotic and the familiar, "Dead Yellow Women" takes the Op inside the den of a Chinatown ganglord. The ganglord and his vassals are smuggling weapons for their countrymen's war against the Japanese 10,000 miles away. Another Oriental appears in "The House on Turk Street." Russians (unsympathetic czarists who get handled roughly by their Marxist-inclined creator) appear in "When Luck's Running Good," "Couffignal," and "The Farewell Murder." In *Falcon,* one of the questers for the black bird, Joel Cairo, comes from the Levant, and two of the gangsters in "The Whosis Kid" are European. Hammett's fertility introduces other kinds of variety. If criminals come to San Francisco from different places, they also bring different purposes and methods. Hammett has both the knowledge and the versatility to portray many different sorts of crime. The killer in "Tom, Dick, or Harry" (1925) is a female impersonator, as is the kidnapper in "The Gatewood Caper." Lovers perpetrate the mischief in "Who Killed Bob Teal?" Professional gangsters work their wiles in "Turk Street," "One Hour" (1925), "The Big Knockover," and *Red Harvest.* Crime in "Couffignal" and "This King Business" is organized along military lines, the armed raiders in each story keeping several options wired by mounting support systems and devising contingency plans.

Though brilliant, these plans fail. Nowhere does Hammett make crime romantic or heroic. Failure to cope as adults carried the Whosis Kid and his later incarnation, Wilmer Cook of *Falcon,* into the underworld. Lured by the glamor of crime, headstrong young women from good homes find squalor, fear, and death. Crime corrupts, turning a gentle-looking old woman into a witch in "Turk Street" as soon as it eats through her benign facade:

> I looked at the old woman again, and found little of the friendly fragile one who had poured tea and chatted about the neighbors. This was a witch if there ever was one—a witch of the blackest, most malignant sort.

15

Perhaps crime ensnares Hammett's women more tightly than it does his men. In "The Tenth Clew," "Silver Eyes," and *Falcon,* love both softens the heart and improves the morals of a female crook: women in each story fall in love with men they had set out to use. But their way is blocked. Having opted for crime, they can no longer summon the outgoings of love. Sometimes, their collaborators won't let them. Crime hampers love; the female crook who wants a straight life in "Silver Eyes" finds herself so deeply enmeshed in crime that her self-preservation demands her killing her innocent lover. At one point she says, "You know how crooks are: everyone in the world is either a fellow crook or a prospective victim." Love hasn't a chance in a world of hustlers and suckers. With everybody looking to exploit everybody else, treachery and lies become norms of daily life. Lovers who are also partners in crime betray each other in "The Creeping Siamese" (1926). A story of wild love, "Woman in the Dark" shows how fugitives and lawbreakers forfeit the benefits of safety, security, and due process. To protect themselves, the story's two main characters, Luise Fischer and the man called Brazil, must depend on people they don't trust and do things they don't want.

How accurate are these insights into criminal behavior? Vincent Starrett said of Hammett, "There is no other writer in the country with his knowledge and experience of criminal folkways."[11] These folkways and the subculture they define refer to losers and misfits, drifters and incompetents. In a 1923 essay-sketch called "From the Memoirs of a Private Detective," Hammett said, "Few criminals of any class are self-supporting unless they toil at something legitimate between times," adding, "I have never known a man capable of turning out first-rate work in a trade, a profession, or an art, who was a professional criminal."[12] People drift into crime as a last resort. They would prefer honest work. They would also prefer the order and neatness of a regular routine. But the distrust shadowing crime rules out all civilized values. Because the criminal always faces the threats of arrest, beating, and death, he can't trust anybody. There is no honor among Hammett's thieves. Animal survival at any price has overwhelmed all. Thus life is a jungle, and crime, the most savage, self-defeating activity of all. "Everybody is trying to slit everybody else's throat," says a crook of his counterparts in "Nightmare Town."

Their small range of choice makes criminals dull and predictable. A shrewd detective can outmaneuver a crook easily. Knowing how distrust and fear have undermined all human ties in Personville's underworld, the Op sets up a meeting of the town's leading gangsters. The trouble he stirs up at the meeting leads to a battle in which many of the gangsters die. Thus the Op fights crime without raising a finger. With the same ease, Spade sets the searchers for the black bird against each other. Greed has blinded them. The speed with which they go for each other's throats shows them hurting each other far more than the police and the courts would.

Criminals also outdo lawmen in the hurt they inflict on each other in "Turk Street," "Whosis," "Nightmare Town," and *Red Harvest*. Here is free enterprise gone berserk. What looks like freedom really denies freedom, the politics of the jungle blocking all creative interchange. Iva Archer, a faithless wife worried about her husband's possible faithlessness in *Falcon*, follows him the night he gets shot. The title, "The Big Knockover," refers to the thieves' corpses littering San Francisco after the thieves are betrayed by their paymaster. "I'm tired of walking into roomfulls of butchered crooks," says a policeman of the carnage. Often no treacherous paymaster or aide is needed; the felon betrays himself. In "Turk Street," a criminal instigates the action that causes his death. The culprit in *The Dain Curse* suffers greater injury from a bomb he plants in his room than those the bomb was intended to destroy. Evildoers in "Eloise Morey" and "The Golden Horseshoe" destroy suicide notes that would have cleared them of guilt. "The Green Elephant" (1923) tells of a Seattle grifter whose lucky find of a quarter of a million dollars in stolen money fills him with panic and dread. Lacking the nerve and the toughness to enjoy his windfall, he moves from hotel to hotel, loses sleep, and conjures up imaginary foes waiting to ambush him. Not until he is accidentally arrested in Spokane does he relax. A moral anecdote, "The Green Elephant" claims that criminals can't enjoy themselves; denatured by crime, the haunted ex-counterman takes his valise of money to bed with him and holds it "in a protecting embrace . . . not unlike a bridegroom's." His isn't an isolated case. There's not a happy criminal in Hammett. Criminals always need more power and money to replace the security and love they have forfeited. Always threatened by fear and hunger, they build walls around themselves.

Sometimes their prisons look like palaces. Casper Gutman knows the benefits of privation. Would owning the falcon improve his lot? He already lives well, spends lavishly, and moves freely around the

17

world. His seventeen-year search for the black bird has given him an important root-source of energy and purpose. To take away his dream would diminish him. Perhaps the very knowledge that the bird lies perpetually out of reach gives it its luster. A fantasy bird suits him better than a material one. How would he infuse his life with intrigue if the bird moved from the realm of mystery into that of fact? How could he recruit aides? prevent the aides from stealing the bird? Criminals in Hammett lack coping power; the closest Hammett comes to portraying a Moriarty or Fu Manchu, in "Dead Yellow Women," never leaves his Chinatown lair. Had Gutman the skill and the drive, he'd be doing honest work. While appearing to enrich him, his long search for the bird wastes him. Spade's nonchalant reaction to the news of his murder, "He ought to have expected that," raises a moral and psychological issue. Perhaps Gutman not only expected his murder, but, rather, welcomed it, having tired both of being excluded from workaday life and sustaining a fiction indefinitely. Seventeen years of chasing a phantom can be exhausting. If he wasn't courting punishment from Wilmer Cook's bullet, he could have been looking for a way to end the frustration of empty-handedness. Several times in the canon, Hammett uses the device, popular in Renaissance drama, of the biter-bit to convey the criminal's lonely auguish. Jacob Ledich, the archtraitor in "Zigzags of Treachery," betrays himself by giving the Op incriminating information in a moment of false security. William P. Kenney shows how Mimi Wynant Jorgensen, in *Thin Man,* loses everything when trapped by *her* own device:

> Mimi discovers . . . that she is herself the victim of deception, for it turns out that her second husband, Chris Jorgensen, is a bigamist. Further, Mimi's greed and her willingness to practice deception toward others leads her to become involved in a scheme with the murderer of her former husband, in which, once again, she turns out to be herself the victim of deception.[13]

II

What other writers grope for, Hammett knows instinctively. He doesn't narrate. Instead, he makes things happen to people. Then he makes us wonder where the excitement came from and what it meant.

There is little in his plots to stretch on the rack of literary theory. Hammett puts forth a personal vision that expresses itself in movement and conflict. There is little moral struggle, the characters having already lost their battles with conscience. Before they come to us, they have decided to rob, deceive a husband, wife, or business associate, steal—even kill for—the falcon. Hammett heightens but won't brood or analyze, showing the effects rather than the development of psychological drama. Vivid in both conception and execution, these effects translate well to radio and screen.

Walter Blair's reference to "objective dramatic narrative method"[14] in Hammett conveys much of the flavor and force of Hammett's surface realism. He forgoes psychic depth to describe fast-moving action in well-drawn settings. Tension comes from the accuracy of detail and intensity of observation he lends to the building plot. Dorothy Parker has shown how his refusal to editorialize, even sometimes to make connections, forces readers to find their own way: "He does his readers the infinite courtesy of allowing them to supply descriptions and analyses for themselves," said Parker in the *New Yorker* in April 1931; "he sets down only what his characters say, and what they do."[15] Parker is right. Hammett avoids giving insights into his characters' thoughts and feelings in order to compel greater reader participation. The Op reacts neither morally nor emotionally to the twin discovery of a corpse alongside him and the apparent murder weapon, an ice pick, in his hand when he wakes from a drugged sleep in *Red Harvest*. His composure creates a high degree of intensity, yoking form to content while forcing the reader to question motives. But it also blocks expansiveness. If Hammett's people change or grow, they keep it to themselves. Rarely do we see a character converted or reborn. Experience teaches little in Hammett, even the experience of terror, as a Tacoma businessman named Charles Flitcraft shows. In Chapter 7 of *Falcon,* Spade tells how a beam that dislodged from a construction site fell and struck the sidewalk next to Flitcraft. His near-accident showed Flitcraft the chance ordering of the universe; had the hurtling beam landed a few inches off its mark, it would have killed Flitcraft. His narrow escape from death shook him deeply. On the spot, practically, he decided to leave his family and begin anew. But color and urgency drained quickly from his rebellion. Within a few years, he had carved out the same suburban niche in Spokane that he had left in Tacoma: "He had settled back naturally into the same

19

groove he had jumped out of. . . . He adjusted himself to beams falling, and then no more of them fell, and he adjusted himself to them
not falling," Spade ends the story. Character is fixed. The Marxist
belief that quantitative changes lead to qualitative ones doesn't apply
to all imaginative literature written by Marxists (unlike the Marxist-
inspired plays of Bertolt Brecht, which argue man's changeability and
perfectibility).

Static characters, rather than fluid ones, indulge overmastering personal drives and participate in tragic clashes of will. Much of this
strong sense of purpose infiltrates detective work. Detectives are
proud, determined people. In portraying them, Hammett gives an intimate inside look at their profession, showing how to collect and read
evidence, how and when to badger a suspect, how to win a witness's
confidence, and how to survive in the field, which includes fighting
both with and without weapons. The reviews of crime fiction he wrote
for the *Saturday Review of Literature* from 1927-29 stress this very
point. Often, the detective-turned-reviewer will complain that his
author has flubbed his facts; the author may not know the kind of en-
try wound made by a bullet of a certain caliber; he may know nothing
of investigative procedure. The last paragraph of Hammett's review
of William Johnson's *The Affair in Duplex 9B* claims, "Neither he
[the Assistant Director Attorney assigned to a case] nor the detectives
working with him show any signs of ever having been employed in
police affairs before." Accordingly, the sleuth in Lyon Brock's *The
Kink* "stalls around till things solve themselves. Even when he gets
hold of a mysterious automobile's license number he takes no steps
tracing it through the Metropolitan Police register, apparently not
knowing that such an affair exists."[16]

Hammett's first-hand knowledge of crime-stopping gave American
detective fiction both a freshness and a command it never enjoyed
before. The narrative drive resulting in part from his brisk, colorful
documentation has also earned him acceptance as the founder of
modern American detective fiction—the tough, realistic mystery
centering on a lonely, cynical private eye. Other honors have followed. George Grella calls him "the most important American detective
writer since Poe." According to Raymond Chandler, who saw him as
Black Mask's "ace performer," he "demonstrated that the detective
story can be important writing." Joe Gores, in his Author's Note to
his 1975 novel, *Hammett,* takes his cue from Chandler: "In such

novels as *The Maltese Falcon* and *The Glass Key,* Samuel Dashiell Hammett (1894-1961) elevated the hardboiled detective story he found in the pulps from a minor form of popular entertainment into literature.'' Noting his wit, stamina, and earthy originality, Ross Macdonald charts the course of his literary trailblazing: "Hammett was the first American writer to use the detective-story for the purposes of a major novelist, to present a vision, blazing if disenchanted, of our lives." This fiery disenchantment has sparked admiration in Europe, André Gide calling *Red Harvest* "a remarkable achievement, the last word in atrocity, cynicism, and horror."[17]

Though most of Hammett's commentators admire his style, plots, and incidents, they sometimes split on the questions of aim and method. (One critic even compares the opening pages of *Falcon* to those of Joyce's *Ulysses.*)[18] Each of the novels has its proponents and detractors. Each adds it share to a vision of America undergoing fast and widescale change. It is the causes and meanings of this change that have provoked different interpretations. Ross Macdonald explains Hammett's main subject as the displacement of frontier energy in the modern city. The feature of the metropolis David T. Bazelon stresses is that of work. Bazelon sees Hammett's chief concern as "the industrial way of life" and "the ascendancy of the job in the lives of Americans." A. Alvarez, looking beneath the concrete skin of the consumer urban state, puts politics at Hammett's animating core: "His best novels, *Red Harvest* and *The Glass Key,* are not really detective stories at all. They are political; they are about what happens and how it feels when the gangsters take over."[19]

Each of these critics seats Hammett's artistry in the city, regardless of differences in emphasis. Though, as has been seen, his vision of depravity extends beyond the American megalopolis, urban malaise underlies much of the canon. The fictional Hammett's pronouncement on vice and corruption describes the San Francisco of the Op stories as accurately as that of Joe Gores's novel; "Every illegal activity in the book is going on right now in San Francisco—gambling, bookmaking, prostitution, protection . . . Anything—*anything*—is for sale here. Any anybody."[20]*Red Harvest's* Personville, or Poisonville, offers all these activities and, with them, police graft, bootlegging, and mob violence. *The Glass Key* accepts this degradation, its main characters consisting of city bosses, their aides, and their rivals, all of whom want to control the rackets rather than wipe them out.

21

Hammett's vision darkened during the two years dividing *Red Harvest* and *Glass Key*. Even though the latter work contains less bloodshed, its violence is more personal and closely felt, stemming from beatings rather than bullets. Poisonville's local czar, furthermore, may have controlled a senator; in *Glass Key* the murderer *is* a senator. But these differences matter less than the similarities linking the two works, both of which make murder coterminous with business and politics. Family and friendship, sexual and divine love, have all given way to greed. The restraints and the faith in due process built into traditional cultures have no force in America's open society, as Hammett portrays it throughout his writing. Free enterprise has, indeed, gone berserk when a democratic people take what they like without regard to others, particularly when the others are immediate family. In *Red Harvest* and *Glass Key,* fathers kill their sons to gain power; *Dain Curse* includes a woman who murders her sister in order to marry the sister's husband and then blames the murder on her victim's small daughter. Casper Gutman sacrifices his surrogate son to the police and talks his natural daughter into jabbing her stomach with needles (as part of the ruse of being drugged)—all for the sake of the mysterious bird. Rhea Gutman's presence in *Falcon* carries weight. That her father has been searching for the bird for as long as she has been alive shows the extent of his obsession; the bird means more to him than any child. Family ties snap under the pressure of greed in the shorter fiction, as well. Betrayal by a brother leads to a boxer's death in "His Brother's Keeper" (1934). Finally, a grifter named Paddy the Mex is killed in "The Big Knockover." The first page of "Knockover's" sequel, "$106,000 Blood Money," introduces Paddy's brother. But the brother has come to San Francisco to win the reward money for capturing the mastermind behind the big heist, not to avenge Paddy's death.

A milieu in which the family can't check greed will also discount spiritual and intellectual values. Though Hammett sets much of his work in the Bay area, only twice does he mention the University of California, located in nearby Berkeley. The Judeo-Christian tradition has dwindled even further. The only religion Hammett displays is the cultism of "The Scorched Face" and *Dain Curse.* The leaders of both cults—named, curiously, Hador and Haldorn—pry money from their devotees by preying on their fears. Highly theatrical, the cults include a giant's helping of sex in their salvation programs. Nor do they

22

shrink from blackmail or even murder to keep the money flowing in. Chapter Twelve of *Dain Curse,* which discusses the aims and methods of the Temple of the Holy Grail, is called "The Unholy Grail." The failure of traditional religion to carry into and cleanse Hammett's crime-ridden cities reaches fullest expression in the falcon. Originally a token of love and religious devotion, the bird has found its way aboard a pirate's ship, into the gutters of Paris, and, most recently, into a private home in Constantinople, in Turkey, land of the infidel.

One of the few satisfactions offered by rough, wild societies is that of getting even. Hammett's characters love exacting revenge, even outside the urban inferno. That timeless revenge story set in the Montana back country, "The Man Who Killed Dan Odams," ends on a strong retributive note. The fugitive tells his hostess that his slaughter of Dan was "fair shooting." Yet, in his deepest heart, he knows that fairness isn't the issue. Survivors of victims usually seek revenge. The fugitive's last words to the widow who ordered his death, "Good girl," spoken "clearly," endorse her revenge-taking. Like Oedipus, he has sought punishment, trekking through mud and over mountain rock to die by the same vigilante justice that put a bullet into his victim a week earlier. Justice is squared again at the end of "The Golden Horseshoe," where the Op arrests and helps sentence a man for a crime the man did *not* commit when it becomes clear that evidence is lacking to sentence him for the crime he *did* commit. Finally, Spade's "turning over" the woman he loves, Brigid O'Shaughnessy, because, "When your partner is killed, you're supposed to do something about it," regardless of what you thought of him, represents Hammett's most famous example of Old Testament retribution. Freeing any murderer would violate both Spade's professional code and his instincts. "It's not the natural thing," he insists; not only the detective working on the case but rather "every detective everywhere" suffers when a murderer is identified and then set free.

Where does murder reverberate most deeply? To ask this question is to go back to the problem of isolating Hammett's bailiwick within the modern American city. Is his commanding center politics? work routine? frontier candor confused by the megalopolis? These questions call for a look at aesthetic tradition. As has been said, Hammett is usually credited with having founded the hardboiled school of detective writing. Nolan's *Dashiell Hammett: A Casebook* assesses his contribution to fictional crime: "With the publication of . . . *Red*

23

Harvest, early in 1929, a new style of detective writing was launched in America: bitter, tough, unsentimental, uncompromisingly realistic, reflecting the violence of its time."[21] Violence smashes families and friendships, careening through Hammett's back alleys, dives, and joints with their scurvy underworld figures. Plenty of fists, blades, and cordite fumes lace the sea air of Hammett's west coast; plenty of murderous schemes are hatched by the socially prominent. This violence is contagious. In *Red Harvest,* the Op complains that he's going "blood-simple," like Personville's natives. He does go blood-wild in "Knockover," participating in a free-for-all with orgiastic glee:

> It was a swell bag of nails. Swing right, swing left, kick, swing right, swing left, kick. Don't hesitate, don't look for targets. God will see that there's alway a mug there for your gun or your blackjack to sock, a belly for your foot.

But only rarely will he answer violence with violence. He, Spade, and Nick Charles of *Thin Man* usually reach their conclusions through legwork and reason. Rather than bashing skulls, they track down leads, study evidence, interview witnesses, and discuss their cases with the police. Robin Thin's policy of exchanging information with the police applies to Hammett's other detectives: "In the long run a private detective is wiser in cooperating with the police than in competing with them," says Thin in "A Man Named Thin." A detective is a manhunter; he has to catch criminals and then produce enough evidence in court to convict them. No good detective will overlook an investigative resource. Thus *Red Harvest,* steeped in gore as it is, includes scientific techniques of detection. "I'm going to have a gun expert put his microscopes and micrometers on the bullets" found in his client's body, says the Op in Chapter 7. His reference to ballistics is entirely in character. The same man who smashes and kicks his way through a roomful of thugs in "Knockover" gives an academic overview of crime-fighting in "House Dick" (1923) that sounds more like formalistic English literary detection than American hardboiled:

> From any crime to its author there is a trail. It may be . . . obscure; but, since matter cannot move without disturbing other matter along its path, there always is—there must be—a trail of some sort. And finding and following such trails is what a detective is paid to do.

24

Sometimes, the Op thinks more about ethics than about technique. He will try to salvage and protect what is best in people rather than punishing them for their mistakes. In "The Scorched Face" (1925), he says, "A couple of dead ones . . . and live ones got mixed up with Hador of their own accords, but . . . don't stop being human beings on that account." Later in the story his compassion rises to that of Ross Macdonald's Lew Archer. Not only does he perceive degrees of guilt; he will also act on his perceptions, protecting those not strictly innocent but more foolish than wicked. His view of justice, furthermore, includes the families of the jailable. Unlike Spade, he can bury guilt as well as punish it. His compassionate morality gains much of its force from not being discussed. No moral crusader, he doesn't curb pain by affecting the tight-lipped mannish stoicism or elaborate casualness so common to his fictional breed. Rather, he assesses people's needs honestly and fully. Rarely has this humanity been credited either him or his creator. In the following passage, from "Scorched Face," his generosity and foresight defuse the damaging possibilities of a case he has just broken:

> If tomorrow's papers say that a flock of photos were found in this house after the fireworks, there's going to be a fat suicide list in the next day's papers, and a fatter list of disappearances. . . . We know this much about the photographs—two women have killed themselves to get away from them. This is an armful of stuff that can dynamite a lot of people, Pat, and a lot of families.

Op's instinct for the jugular displays itself no more often than his instinct to protect. Basically, this squat, anonymous middle-aged gumshoe is a curbside reasoner, collecting and weighing evidence with professional skill. The key difference between him and his British counterparts is that he does his reasoning in mean streets and police stations rather than in the laboratory, the country-house library, or the Duke's castle. Leonard Moss's assessment of him shortens the gap between him and the methodical, highly informed sleuths of R. Austin Freeman, Freeman Wills Crofts, and Dorothy L. Sayers:

> Hammett's most noteworthy character . . . remains primarily a puzzle-solver. When not just stirring things up, the Op adapts venerable investigative concepts to modern police methods. He painstakingly collects facts. . . . In the field he depends upon

careful observation . . . He obtains information by surveillance and by questioning anyone remotely associated with the crime. Finally, he often seeks help from other private operatives, from hotel and police detectives, from hired informants, from taxi drivers and railroad employees.[22]

In this regard, also worth mentioning is Spade's deliberate, painstaking scrutiny of physical evidence. Huge differences obtain between the British mystery of the 1920s and 1930s and the hard-boiled American detective story that developed from the pulps. In several major categories, Hammett is resoundingly American — his emphasis upon professional, rather than private, crime; his portrayal of crime as widespread and cancerous rather than isolated; bitter-sweet finales that bring no tidy resolutions, sudden revelations, or restorations of grace. The Great Wrong Place, as Auden calls the milieu of American crime fiction in "The Guilty Vicarage," has hardly ever been wronger, dirtier, or more bent.

On the other hand, its treatment harkens to classical models. Much of Hammett's technique comes straight from the school of literary detection beginning with Poe and extending through Conan Doyle and Agatha Christie. Violence flares out in an expensive resort home in "Couffignal" that stands about as far from San Francisco as Miss Jane Marple's St. Mary Mead does from London. The anonymity of the detective in Poe's "Thou Art the Man" recurs in the Op. As Cawelti has shown, *Falcon* extends the convention of the hidden treasure, originating in Poe's "Gold-Bug"[23] (and carrying forward in Conan Doyle's "Musgrave Ritual"). Solutions by unexpected means, like the ones in "The Murders in the Rue Morgue" and "A Scandal in Bohemia" return in Hammett's "In the Morgue" (1923) and "Fly Paper." Op's summary comment on his solution in the latter work, "That's the only total that what we've got will add up to," has a logical irrefutability worthy of Sherlock Holmes; like Holmes and Hercule Poirot, the Op puts facts before theories, and he doesn't mix detection and sentiment. The misdirection of the reader's attention in "The Gatewood Caper," "The Tenth Clew," and *Thin Man* rests on devices introduced by Poe and used by Christie in both *The Murder of Roger Ackroyd* (1926) and *The ABC Murders* (1936). Finally, Hammett links Poe's convention of the most obvious place ("The Purloined Letter') to that of the Least Likely Suspect in *Dain Curse* and *Falcon,* where the detective and the culprit have a close tie. Elsewhere, he varies the convention. The mastermind behind the bank robberies in "Knockover" is so shabby and rundown that he escapes the police's notice; nobody, including the Op, suspects this cringing old runt. "The Nails in Mr. Cayterer" introduces a comic variation to the crime of the most obvious place. The information leak that makes a San Francisco businessman blackmailable doesn't originate in China, where the man has secret dealings, but in his own office, with his teenage office boy.

His heavy debt to classic techniques of literary detection doesn't make Hammett a genteel writer of logical exercises misplaced in the urban jungle. It does show that he read widely in his field, thought about what he read, and used Poe's techniques with care and artistic rigor. Unlike Raymond Chandler, he wasn't undermining the crime-puzzle tradition so much as extending it. The vision of depravity he puts forth is too rich and omniform to fit under the umbrella term, hardboiled. His lank, spare idiom didn't rule out sophistication, subtlety, or range. Although he develops his fast-moving action stories without moral commentary, his objective realism cuts deep. Critics have already warned against the practice of labelling him. Steven Marcus refers to "the complexity, ambiguity, and sense of the problematical"[24] permeating his work. Cawelti complains that the common practice of calling him a realist comes from equating realism with violence and toughness. Cawelti doesn't buy the equation. To him, Hammett's so-called realism has been both overrated and misunderstood:

> Is it really the case that a Hammett novel like *The Maltese Falcon,* which revolves around a mysterious age-old treasure, eccentric villains, and complex webs of intrigue, is more "realistic" than the detective novels of Dorothy L. Sayers with their ordinary settings, their relatively plausible motivations, and their rich texture of manners and local color?[25]

The advertising agencies, country villages, and university quadrangles in Sayers, Cawelti continues, have no counterparts in Hammett for tameness and predictability.

Cawelti isn't the only critic who has noted Hammett's bent for the fantastic and bizarre. Discussing Hammett's inventiveness, Frederick H. Gardner claims that the compactness of his man's style darkens and enriches, rather than trivializing, the narratives: "Hammett's style is the opposite of terse. His settings are exotic, and his inclination

27

as a plotter is toward the more intricate and inclusive."[26] As in Joseph Conrad, Hammett's combinations of exoticism and tightness of phrasing create intensity. For the sake of counterpoint, Hammett includes the macabre, the unfamiliar, and the incongruous. A joke may be funny, like the one Eloise Morey plays on herself, but its context is grim. A harmless-looking old man organizes a bank robbery that causes the death of hundreds.

Hammett's belief that weird or ghostly tales must mix the bizarre and the believable helps explain his own fuguelike orderings: "The effectiveness of the sort of stories that we are here concerned with depends on the reader's believing that certain things cannot happen and on the writer's making him feel — if not actually believe — that they can but should not happen."[27] Hammett's art of the grotesque stems from a southern tradition including Faulkner, Carson Mc-Cullers, and Flannery O'Conner. It looks ahead to the city-grown monsters of Nathanael West and Joyce Carol Oates. Crowding too many people into too tight a space and then polluting their air with industrial fumes inhibit normal healthy growth. What emerges is the grotesque. Now Freud relates the grotesque to the uncanny. Its fusion of the familiar and the strange excites dread because it makes us feel unsafe; recognizing that the homespun can be invaded and overtaken by the sinister induces terror. The dissolution of the frontier into the megalopolis, the conjunction of cruelty and kindness, and the infiltration of the macabre by the casual all pulse through Hammett. Sometimes, a grotesque stroke will just miss being funny, as when a tall, thin man named Rounds appears as a corpse in "The Creeping Siamese." Murder in *Thin Man* induces an added shudder for breaking into the festivities of a Christmas vacation. *Falcon* sets up bipolar tensions between Spade's professional devotion and his sexual looseness and between beams that fall and beams that stay in place. Along with Hammett's extending the novel's perimeters to the sixteenth century and to Malta and Turkey, these tensions generalize the danger. Rooting the outlandish in the believable gives the reader a disarming sense of the fundamental wrongness of things. The most reliable and relied-upon structures seem about to dislodge a beam or two and send them hurtling down on us.

The fears roused by the possibility of falling beams build suspense, the manipulation of which Hammett has defined thus: "The essence of suspense is that while it lasts nothing happens."[28] In Hammett,

28

what takes place before us never quite distracts us from the pattern forming in the background. The color and drive of his fiction hides only in part the truth that action in Hammett usually refers to something else. "The key scenes in Hammett," says Ellery Queen, "are not the spectacular bloodlettings, but the quiet, tense interplays of character in dialogue."[29] Sometimes, even dialogue can mislead. The jokes that flit between the Op and Chang Li Ching in "Dead Yellow Women" (1925) don't make the men forget that they're fencing hard—for both information and a psychological advantage. Those who want the most from Spade—Brigid and Gutman—also flatter him the most. What is more, their flattery, centering on Spade's alleged wildness and unpredictability, falls wide of the mark, Spade's slow, unhurried methodicality having already moved to the fore several times in the action. Spade never exposes the inaccuracy and emptiness of the flattery. As has been seen, lies are an everyday reality in Hammett. After recounting the 300-year history of the black bird, Gutman asks Spade, "You begin to believe me a little?" The question says a good deal. Liars themselves, Hammett's people assume they are being lied to. Spade is no exception. He holds back information from the D.A. for the sake of a client who holds back information from *him*. He will even lie to himself if the guilty client, Brigid, tells him a lie plausible enough for him to live with.

The difference between what a character says and what he means constitutes subtext. As the words of Brigid and Gutman (both of whom flatter Spade for the purpose of lowering his guard) indicate, rarely will a Hammett character state his or her exact meaning. When Paul Madvig of *Glass Key* is asked, "Are you going to back the Senator . . .?" he answers, "I think *we* will" (emphasis added). On the next page, he must ask Beaumont twice, "What the hell's the matter with you?" before Beaumont lies, "There's nothing the matter with me." Beaumont does reveal the cause of his worries indirectly, a couple of paragraphs later, when he says of Madvig's senator, a propos of nothing said to him, "Throw him down, Paul. . . . Sink him." Surface action in Hammett may drift far afield from a competing psychological drama. "The shakiness of his hands was incongruous with the steadiness of his voice," Hammett says elsewhere of Beaumont. Body language belies verbal inflection and vocal tone throughout the book. While chewing his cigar nervously, Beaumont will talk with casual politeness. This disjuncture of language from

29

truth, besides undermining the probity of appearances, turns life into dramatic performance. The best bluffer will win the biggest prize; the unseen, the implied, and the whispered outpace what is freely given and directly stated. A writer praised for his solid, factual style, Hammett discredits empirical reality. The harvest of *Red Harvest* is a bloodletting, a denial or negation of fruitfulness; the Dain Curse refers to a legacy that either doesn't exist or exists in an unexpected form; the Maltese falcon is a fake; the glass key appears in a dream; the title character of *Thin Man* died two or three months before the novel begins.

The mannish talk and people in Hammett mask a feminine appreciation of what is indirect, intangible, and unrevealed. Has his archetypal tough guy bypassed life's greatest rewards? Has he reached in the wrong places for the wrong things? At least one of the stories, "Nightmare Town," favors female tenderness over brute male energy. The argument is made symbolically. Steve Threefall, a newcomer to Izzard, defeats his enemies with his spinning, whirling ebony walking stick; the blackness of this source of phallic power, self-protection, and identity conveys both the mystery he poses to the people of Izzard and the unknowability of his strange male force. The flailing stick helps him in Izzard, a wild desert boom town. But when he leaves at the end with his ladylove, he throws it away, recognizing that it won't help him cope with the challenges of normal civilization. Izzard's rowdies and roughnecks have made the town a cultural void. Thus Steve, who, at age thirty-three, is prime for rebirth, and Nova Vallance, whose first name suggests renewal, must go elsewhere. Steve's last display of phallic splendor occurs near the end, as he fights off a gang of assailants on his way out of town:

> Men filled the doorway. An invisible gun roared . . . The stick whipped backward and forward, from left to right, from right to left. It writhed like a live thing—seemed to fold upon its grasped middle, as if spring-hinged with steel. Flashing half-circles merged into a sphere of deadliness.

Steve's farewell to the deadly sandscape of Izzard and his ensuing rebirth, in distant green Virginia, entails his relaxing his frontier individualism. The self-made man must let others serve him; he must learn that love is given, not earned. Steve benefits from these humanizing lessons. He has put himself in Nova's hands. At the end of the story, she is driving out of Izzard with his sleeping head on her shoulder.

A more naturalistic treatment of the limits of maleness comes in the early (1922) story, "The Barber and His Wife." Louis, an athletic barber of ruddy good health, learns of his wife's affaire. His course of action is clear: "There was nothing to think over," he remarks inwardly. "He had a wife. Another man had encroached . . . on his proprietorship. To a red-blooded he-man the solution was obvious." Going straight to the sales office where the man works, Louis bloodies his face. But when he gets home, he sees that his "sensible, manly solution of the problem" has created more problems. Having learned of the one-sided fight in the sales office, the barber's wife has bolted with her lover. Her name, Pearl, with its echo from *Othello*, suggests her great value. Louis threw away a pearl richer than all his barbering tribe because he lacked patience, gentleness, and understanding. (Hammett's identification of the ruthless, acquisitive male ego with blades and scissors predates by five years Virginia Woolf's much more celebrated use of the same symbolism in *To the Lighthouse*.) His proprietorship and his unimaginative policy of framing simple answers to complex problems spell out the shortcomings of the masculinist ethic (and also of the capitalist ethic, the one-time strike-breaker turned Marxist might have enjoyed noting).

Louis isn't a brute clear through. His ability to love Pearl as she deserves shows in his having married her, to begin with; a total dullard would have overlooked her merits. But his pride both in his physique and his prospering barber shop has numbed his heart. Having fostered the worship of material things, his secular, male-dominated society comes under sharp attack. The story begins at the barber's apartment at early morning and ends in the same place at bedtime. This unity of setting and of time—the action covers one working day—reveals that everything and nothing have changed. Though Pearl faces new adventure, Louis stands, literally and figuratively, where he stood that morning. His attempt to heal the rift in his marriage has only widened it. What is worse, the meaning of Pearl's departure has escaped him. The application of muscle to problems calling for imagination and the suspension of judgment can only worsen them. Hammett has infused a richly human truth into his vision of urban disenchantment. Like Steve Threefall's victory over Izzard, Louis's self-defeat reflects the truth that civilizations, in contrast to societies, require a balance of male and female principles.

31

III

The female strain in Hammett goes deep. The "purity and concentration"[30] Alvarez finds in his style depends largely on his feminine sensitivity to nuance and texture and on his lightness of touch. The poise of his intense, immaculate prose proves that hardhitting English needn't be flat and stark. Their rigor of description and subtle word music lift his stories miles above most other *Black Mask* adventures. Hammett's best work creates a singleness of effect, all of the well-observed details of the plot working together and carrying the action forward to the well-pointed climax. Toning down the swift declarative prose is a good ear for the sound of words, especially in context. An occasional old-fashioned touch, like using the word, "presently," for "soon," or "rooms" for "apartment," will add a measure of reverberance and stateliness.

The broadest summary of both the strengths and weaknesses of Hammett's style comes from Ross Macdonald:

> It has pace and point, strong tactile values, the rhythms and colors of speech, all in the colloquial tradition that stretches from Mark Twain through Stephen Crane to Lardner and Mencken. . . . Still it is a dead pan and rather external prose, artificial-seeming compared with Huck Finn's earthy rhetoric, flat in comparison with Fitzgerald's more subtly colloquial instrument. Hammett's ear for the current and the colloquial was a little too sardonically literal.[31]

Hammett's style, like his plotting, is melodramatic in its tendency to simplify. The hard, metallic edge of his dialogue can foreshorten reality, thinning and draining vim from effects that call for expansiveness. Conversation in Hammett, for instance, rarely makes us feel that we live amid a wealth of possibilities. Remote from the life most of us live and know, many of his dialogues have little relevance beyond themselves; the Op's behavior, for instance, reflecting his inner disposition for but a single moment. The prose of Hammett conveys thinking and being at a limited level.

But what it lacks in range, it makes up for in bite. Hammett describes danger tersely and accurately, using no words that will relax the tension. Depending on the effect he wants, he makes pistols snap, cough, clatter, and roar. Bullets can be sprinkled, sprayed, or poured;

in "Couffignal," a machine gun hurls out "its stream of bullets." Yet these live, hopping images don't numb us. Thanks to his sure grasp of graphic dynamics, Hammett can put us in the middle of a violent action without destroying aesthetic distance when distancing is called for. For one thing, his wonderfully sharp perceptions create original effects out of commonplace materials and ordinary phrasing. The Op calls a police detective in "The Main Death" (1927) "a freckled heavyweight, as friendly as a Saint Bernard puppy, but less intelligent." A more effective tool Hammett uses, often to distance violence, is irony. Alvarez has shown how deadpan prose lets him live with violence without becoming its devil's advocate. "Hammett has a genius, and part of it lies in his ability to make corruption seem normal without quite endorsing it," says Alvarez, before explaining Hammett's detachment as a by-product of style. "His achievement," Alvarez continues, "is to have evolved a prose in which the most grotesque or shocking details are handled as though they were matters of routine, part of the job."[32]

One device Hammett uses to tone down and thus criticize violence is that of parallel structure. Resisting the crescendo, at a time when the action seems to ask for it, creates an incongruity between a dramatic event and its phrasing. The verbal irony caused by the incongruity carries moral judgment, Hammett's refusal to heighten the drama stylistically blunting its heroism. Rather than bestowing import, the balanced sentence rhythms detract. Hammett uses this parallel phrasing in his book reviews as well as in his fiction. In all cases, it conveys disapproval. Of Walter Gilkyson's *The Lost Adventurer,* he says, "The book's plan is ironical. Its execution is not. The result is confusing." He applies the same rhetorical strategy to his review of Jean Stark's *Phantom in the Wine:* "The publisher calls this a defiant and impetuous first novel. . . . The author calls it an ironic romance. The reviewer calls it thinnish melodrama."[33] When used to describe violence in Hammett's own fiction, this balanced cadencing can trivialize excitement and danger. Sometimes, an added detail will sharpen the criticism. The wild energies squandered in a shootout in *Red Harvest* merge with the smoke drifting from a cigarette:

> The machine-gun by the tree fired, haltingly, experimentally, eight or ten shots. Noonan grinned and let a smoke ring float out of his mouth. The machine-gun settled down to business, grinding out metal like the busy little death factory it was. Noonan blew another smoke ring.

33

An even rarer stylistic gift comes in Hammett's ability to write paragraphs whose materials and flow both criticize what is being described. The seemingly irrelevant last sentence in this paragraph from "Dead Yellow Women" conveys the communication barrier between the Op and his female client better than a page of sputtering dialogue and nervous gestures; "It was a restful ride. Neither the girl nor I wasted energy on conversation. My client and I didn't seem to like each other very much. She drove well." The following description of a Chinese wrestler, later in the story, makes the wrestler both a vivid sense datum and an object of mind. The theological slant of Hammett's editorial remark imparts grandeur to the striking image, rather than detracting from it:

> The door was opened by another Chinese. But this one was none of your Cantonese runts. He was a big meateating wrestler—bull-throated, mountain-shouldered, gorilla-armed, leather-skinned. The god that made him had plenty of material, and gave it time to harden.

Often Hammett's style achieves distinction by seeming to ignore it. His mastery of the art of direct statement—the groundplan of his verbal strategy—is a good example. To describe the jerky bustle of a fight, he will use short paragraphs. These staccato thrusts have the suddenness of thrown fists, glinting blades, or gunbursts. Frequently extending less than a full line, they don't express speed and drive so much as they do confusion. And with good reason: violence yanks us from one impulse or impression to the next; nothing coheres, develops, or makes sense. The following excerpt from "Scorched Face" trades shrewdly on the truth that sensation precedes reflection and that, further, a torrent of sensations makes reflection impossible:

> My cheek took fire. My head was a roaring thing, about to burst.
> The silk slid away.
> Pat hauled me upright.
> We started down the stairs.
> Swish!
> A thing came past my face, stirring my bared hair.
> A thousand pieces of glass, china, plaster, exploded upward at my left.
> I tilted head and gun together.

34

A Negro's red-silk arms were still spread over the balustrade above.

I sent him two bullets. Pat sent him two.

* * *

In a little passageway I found Raymond Elwood.

He was sobbing and pulling frantically at a locked door. His face was the hard white of utter terror.

I measured the distance between us.

He turned as I jumped.

I put everything I had in the downswing of my gun-barrel—

A ton of meat and bone crashed into my back.

If the passage implies that Hammett's best stylistic effects are descriptive, rather than analytical, the implication shouldn't mislead us into underrating his skill in deploying his descriptive powers. The massive Chinese wrestler in "Dead Yellow Women," "handsome, brutal" Big Flora of "Knockover," and Casper Gutman all attest to Hammett's ability to portray grotesques with carefully perceived, selected, and arranged physical details. The heir to the throne of Muravia in "This King Business" has the barbaric splendor and indomitability of Conan Doyle's King of Bohemia in "A Scandal in Bohemia":

This Vasilije Djudakovich stood nearly seven feet tall, and that was nothing next to his girth. Maybe he wouldn't weigh more than five hundred pounds. . . . He was a blond-haired, blond-bearded mountain of meat in a black frock coat. . . . His eyes . . . were shaded into a colorless darkness, like water in a deep well. His mouth was a fat red oval among the yellow hairs of his whiskers and mustache.

The skillful modulation of hues and textures in Hammett's verbal portraits needs stressing. The writer of the florid, extroverted description of the future Muravian king could also keep step with the delicately coordinated process of rolling a cigarette in *Falcon* or capture the subtle sweetness given off by the Arizona desert in one of her gentler moods in "Corkscrew" (1925):

The morning warmed as we rode, the sun making long violet

35

pictures on the desert, raising the dew in a softening mist. The mesquite was fragrant, and even the sand . . . had a fresh, pleasant odor.

Repetition sometimes makes a description memorable. Hammett will choose a word, usually a concrete noun both apt and rare, and mention it several times in connection with a person or place, as in a *leit motif* in music. The word, "coulee," names a leading feature of the rough Montana landscape in "Dan Odams." "Bulbs," describing the jouncing fat pods of Gutman, enlivens the paragraph introducing him, along with its cognate, "bulbous." Most of Gutman's future appearances will include the word, too, but in no set sequence, Hammett achieving variety amid the unity won by his special effect. Other sorts of phrasing will help him give his stories a good start. The first words of "Death on Pine Street" (1924) create expectations which the story later fulfills. Appropriately, a strong sensual image, "A plump maid with bold green eyes and a loose, full-lipped mouth," introduces an action that will traffic heavily in sex.

Another story of sexual lust, "The Tenth Clew," contains what is perhaps Hammett's most brilliant moment—his description of the Op trying to keep from drowning in cold, nightbound San Francisco Bay. The Op wavers between sleep and wake as the chopping waves lull and rouse him amid the wail of tormenting fog horns and sirens from nearby boats. The Op's strength and resolve, already lowered by the blow that knocked him into the Bay, leaks into the thick, lowhanging fog and the dark, numbing waters. Impressions blur and recede. Just when blackness is about to overtake him, he rallies with a cry for help. Soon he is taken ashore. Much of the excitement of the extended description of his struggle comes from Hammett's impressionistic technique. As has been said, sensation precedes explanation or analysis. It also promotes immediacy, bringing reported action to the moment of experience. The following rush of impressions, unmodulated by grammatical controls, from "Whosis," drops us in the midst of a wild, bewildering event: "A noise of brakes, shouting voices, broken glass. A woman's scream. Figures moving in the scant space between touring car and taxicab. Both cars rocking. Grunts. Thuds. Oaths." Impressionism is one of Hammett's favorite techniques. "The door to my room split open. Floors, walls, and ceiling wriggled under, around, and over us. There was too much noise to be heard—a roar that was felt bodily." Thus begins the account of an explosion in *Dain Curse.* Rather than saying that a bomb exploded in his room, the Op recreates the mad, lurching sensation created by the exploding bomb. In like manner, he draws the reader into the action of "Couffignal" by noting of a woman, "Something heavy was sagging and swinging in the right-hand pocket of her gray flannel jacket." His not telling us outright that the woman is carrying a revolver lets us discover that fact for ourselves at the same time he does. Touches like this make us feel we are living an experience rather than reading a book.

This vividness is served by a mature sense of judgment and discrimination. Hammett was not bedazzled by the romantic conventions of 1920s popular fiction. "Few men *get* killed," the Op says in "Whosis," adding, "Most of those who meet sudden ends *get themselves* killed." A detective stays alive by avoiding bravado. In *Red Harvest,* the Op wires his agency for help rather than taking on the mob by himself. Dick Foley, Mickey Linehan, and Bob Teal are a few agency operatives he has worked with. Another aide, bullet-headed Detective Sergeant O'Gar of the Homicide Division of San Francisco's police force, has won his respect for "having a lot of sense" and "being comfortable to work with." O'Gar and the Op don't compete for glory; nor do they risk their skins to impress others. A good crime-stopper sees through heroics, distinguishes between the true and the phony, and scorns what Tom Sawyer might call "fancy touches." The underplayed title, "This King Business," typifies both Hammett and his sleuths. A great deal is riding in the story—a nation's sovereignty, the balance of power in the Balkans, three million dollars in indemnity, and several lives. Yet the Op treats his assignment as part of an ordinary day's work. Hammett's treatment, too, like his title, isn't operatic or theatrical; the Op sees himself as a tradesman rather than a crusader. Those who indulge romantic stereotypes he won't take seriously:

> These bankers and deputies . . . are a lot of movie conspirators. Look at 'em! They hold their meetings at midnight, and all that kind of foolishness. Now that they're actually signed up to something, they won't be able to keep from spreading the news. All day they'll be going around trembling and whispering together in odd corners.

Good sense keeps him from being swept into the melodrama. The grandiose, the self-indulgent, and the derivative, he rejects. On the other hand, he both recognizes and honors real nobility. Though ignorant of the language of Muravia's new king, he is moved by the man's presence. The king's chief rival, a heel-clicking general, he had already dismissed as theatrical and spectacular.

The Op says of a murder suspect in "The Creeping Siamese," "Being around movies all the time has poisoned his idea of what sounds plausible." Rating dramatic effect over plausibility does in several of Hammett's people. The scruffy title character of "Itchy the Debonair" (1924) wants to become a gentleman-crook like E.W. Hornung's A.J. Raffles. Itchy's reading of escapist fiction defeats him. The elegant evening clothes he wears for his robberies, by making him conspicuous, soon puts him in the hands of the police; the end of the story finds him under arrest in San Francisco's Hall of Justice. Another small grifter, Tom Doody, runs afoul of his criminal ambitions in "Wages of Crime" (1923). After serving a jail term for a crime he didn't commit, Doody lectures sanctimoniously on moral reform. The deathbed confession of the real robber not only clears Doody but also destroys the basis of his appeal as a public lecturer. One wonders if his flair for drama hadn't betrayed him into playing a convicted bank robber, to begin with. Perhaps Hammett's leading example of romantic stereotype as a test of both judgment and character is the black bird. Whereas Spade holds no special brief for the bird, referring to it as a "dingus," Gutman and Joel Cairo are so besotted that the lure of the bird makes them childish. When Gutman learns that the bird brought to Spade's apartment is a fake, he soon asks Cairo, "his smile . . . a cherub's," to go with him to Turkey in search of the real bird. Cairo's response, "I go with you!" comes as a giggle and a cry. The storybook glitter of hidden treasure has robbed the two men of maturity and control. While preparing to renew their search for the falcon, they have forgotten to protect themselves. The priority that Hammett gives to nearest things tallies the high cost of their mistake. Wilmer Cook, the aide they had earlier agreed to throw to the police, has slipped out of Spade's apartment determined to repay their treachery. Blinded by the false gleams cast by the elusive bird, Gutman is an easy mark for Wilmer's bullet.

These gleams wouldn't blind solid, literal-minded Spade. His survival depends on puncturing the fatuous and the bogus. To Wilmer's pseudo-tough, "Keep riding me and you're going to be picking iron out of your navel,'' Spade answers casually, ''the cheaper the crook, the gaudier the patter.'' He avoids affectations of speech. His sensitivity to language shows in his responding to the phrasing rather than the meaning of his secretary's question, ''On the *La Paloma?*'' ''*The La* is a lousy combination,''' Spade says of Effie's double definite article. Aside from an occasional foray into gangster cant with Wilmer, to show the boy that tough talk doesn't impress him, he keeps his speech pure. Both he and the Op, who finds the clipped speech of his Canadian colleague, Dick Foley, quaintly amusing, avoid double negatives, choose verbs that agree with their subjects, and speak in complete sentences. In brief, neither man conforms to the stereotype of the fictional detective.

Brigid's sentimental appeal, that of the helpless, put-upon woman in need of a protector, tests Spade more deeply than either Wilmer's posturing or the falcon. Although he must hold his breath during Brigid's tearful plea for help (to escape contamination or to stop from laughing? we wonder), he resists it as another attempt to intrude a self-serving fictional stereotype upon reality. Interestingly, his powers of resistance may surpass those of Hammett, who will sometimes use the stereotypes as plotting devices. But, anticipating our objections to the practice, he will also make fun of them while floating them before us. A scene in ''Knockover'' shows the Op slugging one crook after another with a lead pipe as they walk unsuspectingly through the doorway where he is planted:

> This foolishness we were up to wasn't so. It couldn't be happening. . . . You didn't stand in corners and knock down people one after the other like a machine, while a scrawny little bozo up at the other end fed them to you. It was too damned silly! I had enough!

Hammett's scorn for fictional stereotypes as thought substitutes and thus enemies of intelligence reinstates the priority of the immediate and the directly perceived, i.e., nearest things. Yet some home truths come to us from afar. One immediate reality Hammett couldn't discuss openly was sex. Owing to the tight censorship of his day, he had to present sex at a remove, treating it symbolically, discussing it after its occurrence, or muffling it inside a web of evasions, concealments, and inventions. The profit motive absorbs it in *Red Harvest;* drugs and madness cloud it in *Dain Curse;* it flares out in *Maltese Falcon* but wanes and dies in the bleakness of Spade's amoral professionalism; the detective in *Thin Man* is already married. Only in *Glass Key* does it reach romantic fulfillment, Janet Henry and Ned Beaumont leaving town together at the end. Yet Hammett robs their leavetaking of uplift and affirmation. Janet is tearful; Beaumont, brisk, evasive, and perhaps scared. The book's last two sentences read, "Janet Henry looked at Ned Beaumont. He stared fixedly at the door." Nor did he invite her to go to New York with him, mention marriage, or display any eagerness to start their new life. His inexpressiveness is well judged. Sex can kill you dead. To show a woman love is to ask for trouble. Survival in the urban jungle requires toughness, practicality, and clarity of mind. Janet won't get the satisfaction of knowing she has won Beaumont's heart. Feigning indifference and polite surprise when his heart is roused strengthens his facade. But Janet understands the facade and makes allowances for it. She demands no protestations of love and need. So long as she knows that his uncaring facade doesn't square with his feelings, she can enjoy and, to some extent, control him. She knows his needs well enough not to ruin her chances with him. The first time they met, when he was a hospital patient, she began panther-tracking him indirectly. She claimed that she wanted him to like her because of her engagement to Paul Madvig, his best friend. This is a lie. She never intends to marry Madvig. After he helps her father get re-elected to the Senate, she'll drop him. Her interest in Beaumont has nothing to do with Madvig. Had she planned to marry Madvig, she'd not have sought Beaumont's friendship, since a man's bride and best friend, if not natural enemies, usually give each other wide berth. Yes, Janet does want Beaumont to like her, but for herself.

Beaumont's resting in bed as he talks to Janet gives their first meeting a sexual undercurrent, which she keeps stirring. Their next meeting takes place *à deux* at his apartment. No sooner is she inside the door than she asks to see his bedroom. Dodges like this keep sex to the fore without making it an issue. *The Glass Key* generates sexual heat in the absence of sexual overtures. For one thing, beds and bedrooms keep appearing in the action, Beaumont's first two meetings with Opal Madvig, Paul's nubile daughter, occurring with one of them in bed. For another, Hammett loads the book with Oedipal symbolism. Sex and death walk together in *Glass Key*. Opal believes her father to have murdered her lover, and a journalist

40

commits suicide when he thinks his much-younger wife unfaithful. Some of the book's Oedipal moments refer as much to Sophocles as to Freud. Senator Henry's murder of his son enacts the Laius complex, reversing the direction of the famous murder at Phocis. Henry's leaving his son's corpse in the street provokes the same wild outcry from Janet that Antigone made when *her* brother's corpse was neglected. Another notable use of sexual symbolism takes place in "Ber-Bulu," whose main character, once again, is the brutish giant, Levison. The story's climax is the shaving of the long, thick, outthrust beard on which Levison's sweetheart used to swing. The beard turns out to have been the source of both Levison's strength and manly dignity. His beard gone, he can't hide his tiny head. The comic difference between the pealike head and the massive body beneath drives him from the village. Rather than being mocked, he cowers away. The name of the Christian missionary who foiled him, Langworthy, sharpens the sexual context of his self-exile.

But, as *Glass Key* proved, sex needn't lead to shame in Hammett—provided that it is treated carefully. Beaumont's pretense of sexual indifference rouses and holds Janet Henry's interest. A variation of this sexual gamesmanship keeps love alive in *Thin Man,* as Kenney has noted. Nick and Nora Charles, says Kenney, "seem almost as a matter of principle to avoid any direct expression of feeling for each other."[34] This lack of outward show seems to help the marriage. George J. Thompson denies the equation of indemonstrativeness and feeling. To him, the Charleses are a happy couple: "In a world where everyone else takes himself so seriously . . . Nick and Nora's ability to laugh . . . seems very healthy and refreshing."[35] By the fruits of their labors let them be judged. Kenney's observation, that the Charleses have tacitly agreed to avoid expressions of love, points to a truth that promotes healthy laughter. The mind turns to Harold Pinter's imperative, the more acute the feeling, the less acute its expression. Perhaps Hammett, too, believes that the key realities of life must be faced indirectly or with a mask of indifference or reluctance. These realities can be lived, but not discussed. Aware of the value of comic distance, Nick and Nora know that their marriage is too serious to be taken seriously. A trained detective, Nick even has to be coaxed into investigating the mystery of the thin man's disappearance.

Hammett's understanding of this delicate psychodynamic matured in the years between *Glass Key* and *Thin Man.* Whereas Beaumont

41

kept his feelings to himself, Nick uses double meanings, changes of subject, and silence to whet Nora's love. Even in the season of giving, Christmas, he won't tell her he loves her. Instead, he tells her that he married her for her father's money. This unfunny joke conveys the value of negative reinforcement. The game of erotic duplicity he plays with her requires both control and imagination. Only two sensitive people with a deep, loving mutual need would bother to play it, alluding to each other's real or imagined sexual misconduct and stopping just short of direct accusations and confessions of guilt. The first chapter of *Thin Man* ends with Nora mentioning the red-head Nick allegedly wandered off with at a party the night before. Nick's "That's silly . . . She just wanted to show me some French etchings" both bloats Nora's suspicions to unrealistic size and carries them to the snapping point. Nora is silenced. In Chapter 4, Nick takes twenty-year-old Dorothy Wynant into the bedroom of his hotel suite to discuss in private her missing father. When the bedroom phone rings, he won't answer it, making Nora come in from the next room. Why? Nora never finds out if he was too busy with Dorothy to get to the phone himself or if his immobility was a veiled plea for help. She doesn't need to find out. She'd rather be kept off balance than grow complacent. Nick's erotic shadow play confirms his faith in the marriage. He works hard at keeping love aglow, and she knows it. Like him, she plays the game watchfully. When it threatens to lurch out of control—as it does when he says that wrestling with another woman gave him an erection—she laughs and changes the subject. Fifteen years his junior, she can't yet play the game with his skill. But she's learning from his example rather than direct advice. Much of the value of the work strengthening their marriage inheres in its not looking like work.

The throwaway style, the boozy casualness, and the wealth of Nick and Nora don't hide their similarity to most of Hammett's other people: they work hard to get and keep what they want. They also resent the interference of outsiders. Strongly motivated, if not driven, they make things happen. Their earnestly undertaken acts can beget violence, which reverberates into dark places and uncovers deep truths. Thanks to Hammett's clean phrasing and ripe heart knowledge, these reverberations have given rise to an urgency and integrity unique to popular magazine fiction in America.

2

The Mind and Heart of the Short Stories

Hammett's short stories resemble superior television thrillers so closely that they make us ask how an age whose cultural heritage consists mostly of TV could have let so many of them drift out of view. At present, less than half of Hammett's short stories are in print. The Continental Op, the nameless manhunter who reminds people of TV's Frank Cannon, is one of our century's most skilled and fascinating literary detectives. The adventures featuring him move briskly, usually pose an intellectual challenge, and gain focus from well-realized atmospheric effects. The stories' superb visual flow and timing extend to techniques of characterization. Characters identifiable by social class, temperament, and regional background make things happen that both obey artistic probability and describe a crime-ridden society. This combination carries conviction. Only Hammett combines the toughness of Raymond Chandler with the technical brilliance of the mature Ross Macdonald. Literature marketed as mass entertainment, his keen-eyed stories appeal to such a wide range of tastes that they will win the recognition they deserve. Although our age prefers novels to short stories, it also prizes the vividness and control that give the stories their special flavor. Hammett has won too many friends with novels like *Falcon* and *Thin Man* to remain obscure as a short-story writer. *The Big Knockover* and *The Continental Op* both got glowing reviews when published in 1966 and 1974. They deserved this praise. Yet Hammett's short stories remain the least read and least understood of the canon. Given their merit, popularity and then honor will follow in due course.

I

This merit peers through the stories' unforced titles. These fit no regular pattern. Some are flat, like "The Road Home," "It," "The Barber and His Wife," and "Fly Paper." Flatness is a function of a number standing as an adjective in "One Hour," "The Tenth Clew," and "The Nineteenth Murder." Some titles like "The Dimple," "The Scorched Face," and "Woman in the Dark" rivet on an image. Titles like "The Green Elephant," "Dead Yellow Woman," and "The Girl with the Silver Eyes" lend the riveting image hue, as do the titles accorded *The Dain Curse* when it first appeared as magazine installments—"Black Lives," "Black Honeymoon," and "Black Riddle" (the 1924 story, "It," was reprinted in 1952 as "The Black Hat That Wasn't There"). A title can feature the name of a major character, often a troubled one, as in "The Sardonic Star of Tom Doody," "The Joke on Eloise Morey," and "The Gatewood Caper." "Tom, Dick or Harry," first published as "Mike or Alex or Rufus," refers indirectly to the problems of stalking a crook who turns out to be a female impersonator. Another kind of indirection comes in the title, "The Main Death," in which the word, Main, cites Jeffrey Main, whose murder the Op investigates. Obliqueness in a title can refer to a place as well as a person: Couffignal in "The Gutting of Couffignal" is an island retirement village; Farewell is a rural village in California in "The Farewell Murder"; Corkscrew, Arizona, is the setting for "Corkscrew"; the epithet, Nightmare Town, describes another wild desert town (in "Nightmare Town"); "The Golden Horseshoe" gets its title from a cabaret in Tijuana. Some of Hammett's titles with place names in them are more straightforward, as in the San Francisco works, "Death on Pine Street" and "The House on Turk Street." The titles fit no formula. In all cases, though, they refer to a main character, incident, or idea in the stories that follow them; they prepare the reader for important developments; they comment on the action or part of it, as in "Ruffian's Wife" (1925), which highlights

Margaret Tharp's shock at discovering her glamorous rover-husband's cowardice.

The action of a Hammett short story will start in no set way. A shriek piercing the San Francisco fog introduces "When Luck's Running Good" (1923). A bright orange tie worn by Sam Spade's client gets "Too Many Have Lived" (1932) under way. The striking image opening "Woman in the Dark" (1933), the title character appearing on a lonely, windswept road in an evening gown, is also visual rather than auditory. None of these stories includes the Op, and only "Too Many" is a tale of detection. Like it, most of the Op stories begin with the detective interviewing a new client, usually in the presence of a third party who has called the detective into the case. In "One Hour" and "The Golden Horseshoe," the third party is Vance Richmond, a grayhaired, often gray-garbed lawyer who gives the field detective information on a case he wants him to investigate. Usually, the third party, whether Richmond or the nameless Old Man, director of the San Francisco branch of the Continental Detective Agency, having gotten the story moving, need not reappear in it. A good example is "One Hour" (1924), where a stolen car belonging to one of Richmond's clients kills a local printer. The car, which is later found by chance, turns out to have been the murder weapon used by a ring of counterfeiters to protect themselves. Once Richmond justifies legally sending Op out to look for it, he drops out. In "Zigzags of Treachery" (1924), his narrative role goes beyond legality, the deep trouble of his client demanding his appearing three times. Suspected of having murdered her husband, the client goes to jail. Her incarceration causes other problems. The husband's death and its repercussions have weakened her to the point where she must go to the city hospital. But even constant medical care doesn't restore her. In critical condition and failing quickly, she'll die unless the Op finds the real murderer quickly. Though the most likely suspect, she never appears in the action. Hammett, in fact, acted wisely to build the action around her and, especially, to keep her out of it, since her presence would have jarred its emotional balance. The urgency of her losing battle with death loses nothing by being voiced by her worried attorney. Op must not only prove her innocence; he must also do it quickly.

Most often, the Op's chief, the Old Man, will monitor the pre-investigative interview between the Op and a new client. "Dead

45

Yellow Women'' uses this three-way discussion to bring in important background information. But the device is by no means general, Hammett too much the artist to lean overmuch on any single mode to get a story under way. "Who Killed Bob Teal?" begins with the Old Man telling Op about Teal's death and sending him out to investigate it with no third person present at the interview. In "Girl with the Silver Eyes," a phone call from the Old Man breaks the Op's Sunday morning sleep and assigns the Op to a missing person's case. Some stories begin with the Op in conference with somebody other than the Old Man. The Op learns about Harvey Gatewood's missing daughter in Gatewood's office; the Old Man never appears in "The Gatewood Caper." Op's first interview in "This King Business" occurs in the Balkan country of Muravia. The foreign setting incorporates a familiar technique; for as soon as the American *chargé d'affaires* gives the Op the information he has come for, he leaves the story permanently. Perhaps the most inventive beginning of an Op case comes in a story set in San Francisco, "The Creeping Siamese" (1926), where a man dies of knife wounds soon after reeling into the Continental's Market Street office.

A story which shows the benefits of making a flying start is "Woman in the Dark." Though mysterious foreign women appeared in "The Whosis Kid" and "Couffignal," neither stood forward as boldly as Luise Fischer, whose foreignness becomes thematic straightaway. Luise's isolation on a cold, empty landscape sets an ominous mood that Hammett builds on by revealing her background, her lameness, and the incongruity of her evening gown. She goes to the only house in sight, which is occupied by a man and a young woman named Brazil and Evelyn Grant. The scene at Brazil's provides our first sustained look at Luise. But instead of saying that Luise is beautiful, Hammett shows the effects of her beauty, not on Brazil, as might be expected, but upon Evelyn: "The girl [Evelyn] was pretty. Facing her the woman [Luise] had become beautiful." Although an emerging love triangle would detract from the mystery of Luise, the possibility of one makes her more mysterious. The girl-woman contrast has helped Hammett keep his options alive. These options strike roots. He has Evelyn crouch between Luise and Brazil while Evelyn tends Luise's leg; then Evelyn covers the leg before leaving her patient alone with Brazil. At no point in the little drama has Brazil expressed any feeling for Evelyn; he has had no chance. To discover both his

46

response to Luise's beauty and Luise's reason for materializing on the dark, lonely road near his house, we must read on. By manipulating the point of view through which the action is seen, Hammett has committed us imaginatively. Is Luise in danger? Has she endangered others? Have Evelyn and Brazil risked their security by helping her? Both the events of the story's first pages and the angle from which they reach us suggest these questions.

The endings of Hammett's stories show the same care as the beginnings. sometimes, the action peaks to a long recitation, consisting of either the sleuth's reasoning or the culprit's confession of guilt. But Hammett is too much the action-writer to end a story with a long speech. To gain a dramatic, rather than verbal, climax, he will follow the speech with a flurry of movement or a new development, like the sexual temptation of the Op in "Girl with the Silver Eyes" and "Couffignal." The development can be muted. The ending of "Farewell Murder," for instance, fuses Hammett's aesthetics with the morality implicit in denying a murderer the last word. Following the villain's long, detailed account of his villainy is the statement, all the stronger for both its shortness and its standing as a paragraph on its own, "They hanged him." Some of the other Op stories end with this kind of factual report. The last paragraph of "Who Killed Bob Teal?" for instance, explains the outcome of the Op's investigation, matching punishment to degree of guilt in a neat package:

As it turned out, Ogburn went to the gallows, Mae Landis is now serving a fifteen-year sentence, and Whitacre, in return for his testimony and restitution of the loot, was not prosecuted for his share in the land swindle.

The last paragraphs of "The Big Knockover," "What a life!" and "Couffignal," "I was glad it was over. It had been a tough caper," add the detective's personal reaction. The Op's self-mocking farewell to the reader at the end of "Dead Yellow Women" contains an ironical shorthand summary of the emotional drain caused by the case: "I don't mind admitting that I've stopped eating in Chinese restaurants, and that if I never have to visit Chinatown again it'll be soon enough." Not all of Hammett's stories end this well, as "The Whosis Kid" proves. Instead of closing with a factual summary, a moral overview, or a witty, upbeat turnabout, this 1925 story has as its finale a short paragraph-length identification of a minor character.

47

This minor character deserves better treatment. Hammett had painted him so crudely that, knowing he hadn't solidified Billie's existence dramatically, he wanted another try. Like Babe McCloor of "Fly Paper," Red O'Leary of "Big Knockover," and the "big, hair-matted beast of a man" named Levison in "The Hairy One," Billie is a vicious giant. Like him and his outsize counterparts, many of Hammett's unsympathetic figures have a memorable physical feature. The Whosis Kid has crinkled ears; Guy Cudner of "House Dick" has a facial scar; the pupils of Creda Dexter's large amber eyes in "The Tenth Clew" never rest; "a big man with a red face around a tiny mouth" and somebody with a limp, twitching nose cause most of the trouble that flattens Vance Richmond's client in "Zigzags." The tactic of realizing a character physically makes for epithets that supply both quick identification and moral judgment. Thus an oversize felon in "Golden Horseshoe" is known only as Gooseneck, and three robbers in "House on Turk Street" are referred to by the Op as the yellow man, the ugly man, and the red-haired she-devil. But the character with a dominant physical feature needn't be an outlaw. Hammett never introduces Detective Sergeant O'Gar of San Francisco's homicide detail without mentioning O'Gar's bullet-head. The small waiflike heroine just out of her teens is almost always sympathetic and usually gets what whe wants. Pretty, dainty young women under five feet tall befriend the Op in "Dead Yellow Women" and "This King Business"; Nova Vallance, with her "small white face of a child of twelve," leaves murderous Izzard at the end of "Nightmare Town." Descriptions like Hammett's of Nova confirm the benefits gained by the humor character of Ben Jonson and the flat character of E.M. Forster, as Forster describes him in *Aspects of the Novel* (1927). They generate atmosphere; they need no reintroducing; they join moral issue to the appearance-reality dualism. In addition, they needn't look like cardboard. The flatness of flat characters can be hidden more easily in short stories than in novels, where they may have more narrative weight to pull and where their flatness, by remaining longer in open view, becomes more conspicuous.

At its worst, the technique resorts to stereotypes. "House Dick" refers to "the eyes of a congenital killer!" to prepare for the onset of violence. Sometimes, the stereotype is racial. In "The Nails in Mr. Cayterer," Hammett's sleuth, Robin Thin, says that "the mature oriental mind frequently displays quite definite analogies with the juvenile occidental mind.'' Has the jazz-age sleuth forgotten the veneration accorded the old in the Orient? Or does he believe that the old are revered in the Far East because they act like American adolescents? In "Dead Yellow Women," the Op refers to "an unmistakable odor—the smell of unwashed Chinese." Whether Hammett bought these racial stereotypes can't be known. Op's wiliest foe and the one he most respects, Chang Li Ching of "Dead Yellow Women," refutes Robin Thin's claim about the greenness of the oriental mind. What is more, the beauty, courage, and abstract talent of Op's Chinese client, a crack tennis player and successful author of twenty-four years, turns the mind as far from "unwashed Chinese" as it can be turned. Lillian Shan and another Chinese woman in the story with a face "like a tiny oval of painted beauty" give nothing away in good looks to any white woman in the canon. By leaning on racial stereotypes, Hammett seems to be invoking prejudices he doesn't endorse. As such, he talks down to his readers, pandering to responses he rejects himself. Curiously, this moral failing takes root in an artistic one. Hammett only resorts to stereotypes to speed his plots or build suspense. They both replace and shortcut the rigors of conventional plotting. Although they aren't likable, they occur but seldom and they are more than counterweighted by insights that convey respect and even admiration.

Most of Hammett's stories don't need race to mount or hold excitement. The plots of "House Dick," "One Hour," "Turk Street," and "Couffignal" all take unexpected turns, as routine cases in each story lurch suddenly into danger. In "Bob Teal" and "Death and Company," the client is the killer. Both the late date (1931) of "Death" and the guilty client's ownership of a manufacturer's agency stir Marxist undertones. (Culprits in "One Hour" and "Too Many Have Lived" may have also used strikebreakers to straighten out labor trouble.) After murdering his wife in her love nest, the client fabricates a murder plot to misdirect attention from him. Quite possibly, he drove his wife to another man's arms with the same proprietorship that soured the marriage of another capitalist, Louis Stemler, in "The Barber and His Wife." "Tom, Dick, or Harry" and "The Tenth Clew" use the fictional convention of the least likely suspect without inviting a political reading; in both works the killer is in clear view all along, but under a feigned identify.

49

Sometimes Hammett will extend or even change a literary convention. Erle Stanley Gardner has shown how the fictional detectives of the 1930s and '40s reasoned from behavior rather than from physical evidence:

> Many of the clues these days are clues of action. In other words, the detective doesn't find a broken cuff link or a fragment of curved glass at the scene of a crime. Instead, one of the characters *does* something that turns out to be a significant clue.[1]

The culprit gives himself away in "The Creeping Siamese" (1926) by stressing an identification (her accomplice as her husband) that, if true, would need no stress. In "Death on Pine Street" (1924), the least likely suspect draws suspicion to himself by making statements he can't support. His insight into criminal psychology serves the Op better than any number of blood scrapings or fingerprints. Using sex, money, and the romantic stereotype of honor among thieves as smokescreens, the three robbers in "Turk Street" (1924) are all trying to sell each other out. The Op finds himself witnessing a three-sided betrayal that puts forth a vision of hell as bleak as Sartre's in *No Exit* (1944). Each robber distracts the other two by stirring up trouble between them and then assuring them in private of his loyalty. Making and breaking pacts at will, each uses the other two as weapons or as would-be suckers or victims. Reason does help the Op in the story, not in discovering the villians but in avoiding their traps.

One truth the Op always tries to apply to a case is that the solution often lies nearby. As Poe said in "The Murders in the Rue Morgue," the more bizarre the crime, the simpler its detection. (Op's rendition of Poe's dictum, in "The Scorched Face," reads, "The crazier the people you are sleuthing act, the nearer you are to an ending of your troubles.") As has been seen, the robber lives in the same apartment building as his victims in "Tom, Dick, or Harry." The crimes in "Couffignal" and "Farewell Murder" are also inside jobs whose bizarre clues and foreign characters both suggest farflung solutions. Hammett returns to the crime of the most obvious place often. The Siamese characters in "The Creeping Siamese" are just inventions of the killer, who has manufactured romantic stereotypes, like giving his victim a background of foreign travel in Brazil, Kandy, and

50

Vladivostok, to mask a simple story of sexual lust. But motives needn't indicate guilt. Sexual intrigue is the red herring in "Death on Pine Street," where the killer turns out to have been the person closest to the victim at the time of the shooting, even though killer and victim didn't know each other. The killer tries to sidetrack the investigation in "Tenth Clew" with a reference to an event that took place in Paris in 1902, twenty-one years before and some 8000 miles away from the crime. Later in the story, an irrelevancy disguised as an important lead turns up inside a page from a five-day-old Philadelphia newspaper, again with the purpose of misleading the police. The brother-killer in "A Man Called Spade" (1932) puts a letter postmarked Paris near his victim and then draws a Rosicrucian pentagram on his victim's chest.

Exoticism gives way to the drab prose of greed in "They Can Only Hang You Once" (1932). In order to live free off of them, indigent Timothy Binnett tricks his legacy-hungry nephews into believing him rich. Old Binnett didn't spend his last fifteen years earning a fortune in Australia, as he tells the nephews, but doing time in Sing Sing. Perhaps Hammett's leading commonsense expression of faith in nearest things comes in "The Nails in Mr. Cayterer" (1926), where the culprit is Cayterer's fifteen-year-old office boy and not somebody in China, where Cayterer has secret business dealings. Hammett adds the original twist of couching the extortion letter in Cayterer's handwriting. He also plays fair by introducing the mischievous teenager both early, in the story's fourth paragraph, and before any of the other suspects and witnesses. Only the detectives, Robin Thin and his father, enter the action before young Ralph.

II

The center of Hammett's moral world isn't Robin Thin, but the "fat, middle-aged, hard-boiled, pig-headed" *(Red Harvest)* Continental Op. Over a period of seven or eight years, this short, thickset detective appeared in thirty-six stories, eight of which were revised into the novels, *Red Harvest* and *The Dain Curse*. He is a functionary rather than a freelancer. His firm, the Continental Detective Agency, which sends him out on cases, is usually called in when somebody either lacks faith in the local police or wants an investigation kept private. A conservative firm, much of whose business, the Op says in "The

Whosis Kid," comes from insurance companies, the Continental protects its clients. Nor will it or its operatives touch any reward money for bringing a felon to boot. A loyal functionary, the Op tries both to make money for his firm and to safeguard the firm's reputation. He won't accept the flamboyant poet, Burke Pangburn, as a client in "Silver Eyes" till he gets an endorsement from the poet's brother-in-law, a notable mining executive; the Continental fears scandal more than nonpayment.

The Op's soft-spoken chief, known only as the Old Man, has a detachment that worries the Op, as is made clear in "The Scorched Face": "The Old Man, with his gentle eyes behind gold spectacles and his mild smile, hiding the fact that fifty years of sleuthing had left him without any feelings at all on any subject." This coldbloodedness gives rise to humor in an interview with Lillian Shan at the start of "Dead Yellow Women." Whereas his angry Chinese client craves positive action, he, the westerner, is inscrutably impassive. Hammett can mock racial stereotypes as well as use them as plotting devices: "She looked at the Old Man, who smiled at her with his polite, meaningless smile—a mask through which you can read nothing," Hammett says of the exchange. Op's relationship with his white-haired, pink-skinned chief is much more casual than that of James Bond and M. Op doesn't call his chief sir, won't shrink from correcting him, and can relax in his presence; in "The Big Knockover" the two men lunch together. A good judge of talent and a deft handler of subordinates, the Old Man assigns Op to the most demanding cases, lets him handle the cases in his own way, and doesn't clockwatch his progress. This confidence stems from professional, rather than personal, motives. Without a scruple, the Old Man assigns Op to the same case on which another operative, Bob Teal, got killed in "Who Killed Bob Teal?" (1924). Op has good reason to believe him coldblooded.

In ways, the Op is just as opaque as the Old Man. Neither man wastes words; neither lets feelings interfere with a job. But whereas Hammett uses the Old Man more as a plotting device than as a character, he develops the Op much more roundly. This development, though, never extends beyond the framework of detection. Though an ace gumshoe, the Op says little about how he acquired his skills and still less of his off-duty self. "I went home to dream of nothing even remotely connected with crime or the detecting business," he says in "The Tenth Clew." The subject of his dream he never reveals. Once he detaches himself from his job, he scarcely exists for us. Aside from keeping anonymous, he tells nothing of his family, education, or religious beliefs. On the subject of his leisure hours, he is nearly as evasive; the only parts of his private life he shares with us consisting of playing poker or going to prize fights. What he does during the rest of his spare time, he keeps to himself.

His background is just as sketchy. Based on James Wright, the assistant superintendent of the Baltimore office of Pinkerton's Detective Agency and Hammett's one-time chief,[2] Op has worked at detection most of his adult life. His first job with the Continental may have been in their Boston office. We do know that he left the Boston branch of the Continental in 1917 to enlist in the AEF, in which he became an officer. He may have also served in Europe, because he knows some French and German. After returning to civilian life, he worked for a couple of years at the Continental's Chicago branch before being transferred to San Francisco, the site of most of his recorded cases. If merit didn't bring about his transfer, it did account for his sharp rise. At the time he appears to us, at age thirty-five or forty, he has a great deal of executive responsibility; he is still his branch's ace field detective; he earns enough salary both to live in the same apartment building as an M.D. and to play poker an evening a week in fashionable Sea Cliff.

He deserves his good salary and the privileges that go with it. His client in "The Farewell Murder," wanting value for money, doesn't complain about the high price charged for the services of "the best detective I could secure." Nolan has outlined the range of these services and the clientele they attract: "He [the Op] would be hired by insurance companies, businessmen, attorneys, housewives. . . . Mainly, Hammett sent him out to trace killers, investigate robberies, and to find missing or kidnapped persons. But the Op also functioned as a guard, payoff man, house detective, and town-tamer."[3] Nolan's well-judged list can be extended to cover other areas. Op goes to the desert in "Corkscrew," to a country estate in "Farewell," to Mexico in "Golden Horseshoe," and to an imaginary Balkan country in "This King Business." In "Couffignal," he guards wedding presents; he investigates industrial crime in "Bob Teal"; "One Hour" shows him stopping an international ring of counterfeiters; gun-running and the smuggling of Oriental immigrants into the country test him in "Dead Yellow Women"; in "Tenth Clew," he solves a murder. Like most detectives in open societies, he can go anywhere at least once and ask whatever questions he believes will bring him closer to a solution. If he feels that the questions may annoy or anger his witnesses, he asks them tactfully. Social rank or power won't intimidate him. He works for the mighty without quailing or truckling, taking charge of and then controlling interviews with the glaring, bull-headed corporation executive, Harvey Gatewood, and clever, manipulative Bruno Gungen, his art dealer-client in "The Main Death." He also refuses to be distracted by female beauty. Although moved deeply by female crooks in "Silver Eyes," "Whosis," and "Couffignal," in all three cases he apprehends his temptress. The sexual temptation in *The Dain Curse* stems from a virtuous young widow. Again, Op refuses to mix detection and sentiment. Though he does make the widow believe she has turned his head, he enacts the deception in order to speed her recovery from nervous depression.

Able to resist beauty, power, and conquest, he inhabits the moral world of the loner. Sam Spade arrests Brigid for killing his partner, not out of loyalty or grief but "because you're supposed to do something about it." Like him, the Op, living in a world without moral guidelines, makes himself up as he goes along, taking help where he finds it. His self-improvisations, performed on the wing rather than in repose, spell out both the dangers and rewards of living without moral props. "The Op does not resist because it is wrong but because it is unprofessional, and his moral sense confines itself to what either gets the job done or benefits the agency,"[4] says William Ruehlmann. Op has few pangs of social conscience, rating competence over feelings of responsibility for the public welfare. In the area of competence, he scores high, aided by practical intelligence, moral courage, and decisiveness. The traits that Frederick Jackson Turner admired in the American frontiersman, "that practical, inventive turn of mind . . . that masterful grasp of material things . . . that restless nervous energy . . . that dominant individualism,"[5] also describe the Op. Secular and mildly anti-authoritarian, he embodies the frontiersman's Protestant preference for conscience over dogma. His inner strength, self-sufficiency, and knowledge of the details of detection make him both a reasoner and an action hero.

Certain kinds of action, though, he will resist. "The proper place for guns is after talk has failed," he says in "Corkscrew." He both values restraint and has the self-control to practice it. But if he can't avoid fighting, he will gouge, butt, kick, or bite an opponent. He wins one fight by pressing his thumbs in the hollows under a thug's ears; working from the outside in pairs, he breaks the fingers of another thug who is strangling him. He can also fight with a knife or a pistol. According to Nolan's rough tally, he killed fifteen people and wounded about a dozen others during his seven-year career in *Black Mask*.[6] In each instance, he kills and wounds for survival, not pleasure; no glowering sadist or primitive justicer he. Indicative of his sobriety amid violence are his refusal to waste bullets and his practice of reloading at first chance during a gunfight.

He comes closest to voicing a professional credo in "Couffignal":

> Now I'm a detective because I happened to like the work. It pays me a fair salary, but I could find other jobs that would pay more . . . .

> *   *   *

> I like . . . the work. And liking work makes you want to do it as well as you can. Otherwise there'd be no sense to it. That's the fix I am in. I don't know anything else, don't enjoy anything else, don't want to know or enjoy anything else. You can't weigh that against any sum of money.

What the credo leaves out is the energy Op pours into his work. Besides fighting well, he has excellent powers of observation, he collects evidence and reasons from it with skill, he can read the signs of danger quickly and accurately; in "Turk Street," "Knockover," and "Fly Paper," he bluffs his way out of tight binds. The modesty of the following self-assessment from "Zigzags" doesn't smudge the force of the observation: "I'm not what you'd call a brilliant thinker—such results as I get are usually the fruits of patience, industry, and unimaginative plugging, helped out now and then, maybe, by a little luck—but I do have my flashes of intelligence." He did well to mention patience; in "Whosis," he sits in a parked car for nine straight hours waiting for the person he's shadowing to leave a nearby building.

Part of being a good detective consists of avoiding detection. Thus he disguises himself in "House Dick" and uses aliases in "Whosis," "Big Knockover," and *Red Harvest*. In "This King Business," while

55

tailing a suspect, he finds himself tailed. He remains calm. The shadow expert knows he can lose his own shadow. After covering his suspect's exit to block escape routes, he notices that his own tail is very close by. To protect his advantage, he hides in darkness and breathes through his mouth rather than his nose. Mouth-breathing for the sake of silence is merely one stratagem practiced by this highly trained specialist. In missing persons cases, he gets photographs and handwriting samples. He interviews the missing person's family, friends, acquaintances and/or colleagues. He will also get the license plate numbers and, if possible, the engine numbers of cars owned or driven by people connected with the case he's investigating, missing persons or otherwise. In "The Gatewood Caper" (1923), he writes down the license plate number of a passing car with his hand in his overcoat pocket to ward off suspicion. Again for self-protection, he destroys an office memo dealing with his assignment right after reading it; "there's no wisdom in carrying around a pocketful of stuff relating to your job," he reasons in "Whosis," knowing that if caught by the suspect he's tailing, he's sure to be searched.

As this reasoning shows, a detective needs good judgment as well as muscle, thoroughness, and quickness of mind. "Fly Paper" shows the Op's judgment working to good advantage. Taking the long view, he won't arrest two people conspiring to defraud his client in the hope that they will lead him to the missing person, his client's daughter. His words to the manager of the building where the conspirators stayed incorporate a useful technique for coaxing information out of a reluctant witness—convincing the witness that his or her interests chime with yours: "I'm not going to make any trouble for you," he assures the hotel manager. "But if they've blown I'd like to know it, and I reckon you would too." He gets the information he came for straightaway. At other times, he'll bully a witness, or ask a few well-chosen questions to build psychological pressure and then keep silent, or tease information out by pretending to know more than he does. These techniques don't always work. A balky witness might panic and strike out with whatever is at hand. Thus he acted wisely in learning how to do medical repairs—like cleaning and stanching a wound or applying a tourniquet. In "Couffignal," he runs cold water on a twisted ankle to stop the swelling. He can also treat ailments not caused by sharp physical contact. His diagnosis of the symptoms of chronic arsenic poisoning in "Fly Paper" shows him to have dabbled

56

enough in internal medicine to protect against subtler forms of violence.

Not all this expertise is self-directed. He also protects his clients and witnesses. The protection can take many forms. In "This King Business" he protects the material interests of somebody who lacks the seasoning to look after them himself. Though prizing competence, he also takes a broad, warm view of it. He tempers his actionism with a compassion that can rise to self-sacrifice. Not only will he console someone in straits. Suspending moral judgment, he will even tend the wounds of the guilty. In "The Golden Horseshoe," he dresses the bullet-shattered arm of the man he has just bested in a shootout (Spade, too, dresses the wounded arm of the murderer in "They Can Only Hang You Once"). Moral judgment fuses with compassion at the end of "Death and Company," where he scolds the villain while tending to his wounded leg. Nor does he expect thanks or praise for his ministrations. No reformer, he takes the world on its own sullen terms. He has the magnanimity to value compassion and honor for themselves. Put simply, he enjoys helping people relieve stress. All the more impressive for lacking roots in any received social ethic, Op's compassion helps fit him to Raymond Chandler's archetype of the American literary detective as set forth in "The Simple Art of Murder": "He must be a complete man and a common man and yet an unusual man. . . . He must be the best man in his world and a good enough man for any world."[7]

Though squat and pudgy, the Op stands tall.

III

Most of Hammett's short fiction gives joy. Nearly every story will display a special skill—a memorable characterization, a surprise ending, a demonstration of brilliant reasoning. What is more, even Hammett's early stories will combine one of these skills with outstanding plot construction.

The early work, which often deals with small grifters defeated by grandiose ambitions, e.g., Tom Doody, Itchy, and Joe Shupe of "The Green Elephant," rarely foreshadows their robust, driving successors. The style in the stories published between 1922-24 often smacks of the dry, thinned-out gruel found in the scientific British detective fiction of the day. The range in modes and settings in the early stories also shows Hammett groping for his subject. Although the stories test his skill with setting, dialogue, and atmosphere, they reflect a growth more rhetorical then thematic; Hammett knew his trade before learning his art. Not until the emergence of the Op in late 1923 does his work take on the sinew that both energized and shaped mature stories like "Dead Yellow Women" (1925), "This King Business" (1928), and "The Farewell Murder" (1930). Nolan finds this sinew and sharpness already present in the 1922 work, Hammett's fourth published story and his first in *Black Mask,* "The Road Home." A detective hired to find a killer finally runs down his man in a South Sea jungle. After the man escapes into the bush, the detective follows, perhaps drawn by the offer of a share in "one of the richest gem beds in Asia" if he frees the man. Here is what Nolan makes of the unresolved action: "The reader is left with the hint that perhaps the detective *will* be corrupted upon sighting the jewels. Thus, Hammett's career-long theme of man's basic corruptibility is reflected here."[8] This well-attested corruptibility may also include the truth that crooks in Hammett don't share; they betray each other. If the Asian gem bed Barnes mentions even exists, it may be serving to lower the guard of the detective. Barnes has already killed one man. There's little reason to think he'd shrink from killing another, especially with his freedom in the balance. As Spade will remind two murderers, they can only hang you once.

"When Luck's Running Good" (1923) introduces an early incarnation of *The Glass Key's* Ned Beaumont, the sympathetic gambler-hero who takes a terrific pounding. The story's Russian characters and the device of confusing gunfire with the sounds of a thunderstorm both recur in "Couffignal" (1925). But the story's most important apprentice-work comes in the Gothic effects, some of which permeate the plot: A helpless, put-upon heroine lives in a remote mansion secured by shuttered windows and heavy bolted doors and also guarded by large, fierce dogs, memorably described as "lithe, evil shapes . . . with flashing, dripping jaws." The heroine's oppressor, a sleek villain who speaks in a measured, bookish style, also browbeats his dim-witted, muscular servants, inheritors of centuries of slaves' mentality. Judging shrewdly, Hammett shed most of these lurid effects in his Gothic thriller, *The Dain Curse* (1929), making the villain American, not Russian, and putting the building where the heroine is stowed right in San Francisco.

A work that prefigures Hammett's mature stories more accurately than "Luck" is "Zigzags of Treachery" (1924). This police procedural shows the Op working both alone and with other detectives. It also controls the jagged rhythm of alliances being made and broken at will; the Op's involvement in the network of deceit giving the action a reliable reference point. The intimate inside look "Zigzags" gives at techniques of criminal investigation, thanks to its narrator-sleuth, nearly makes it a primer on detection. Here are a few of the insights the Op provides. All will recur in the later fiction in expanded, dramatized form; parts of the first and second passages will also recur in paraphrase or summary:

> There are four rules for shadowing: Keep behind your subject as much as possible; never try to hide from him; act in a natural manner no matter what happens; and never meet his eye. Obey them, and, except in unusual circumstances, shadowing is the easiest thing a sleuth has to do.

*   *   *

> We got not another word out of her; and that is the only way in the world to beat the grilling game. The average suspect tries to talk himself out of being arrested; and it doesn't matter how shrewd a man is, or how good a liar, if he'll talk to you, and you play your cards right, you can hook him—can make him help you convict him. But if he won't talk you can't do a thing with him.

*   *   *

> A man who is a fair shot . . . naturally and automatically shoots pretty close to the spot upon which his eyes are focused. When a man goes for his gun in front of you, you shoot at *him*—not at any particular part of him . . . . You are more than likely to be looking at his gun, and in that case it isn't altogether surprising if your bullet should hit his gun.

The Op needs plenty of help in "House Dick" (1923), an early story that features both reason and violence. The story begins with a puzzle and ends in a gunfight at a gangster dive. The Op's concluding explanation pieces together the loose bits while toning the story to a peaceful, rationally satisfying finale. The case begins fitfully when three murder victims tumble out of a clothespress, one on top of the other. For variety, each victim dies differently—through strangulation, stabbing, and a blow to the head. Op has few clues or leads. Robbery was no motive; the victims seem to have been unacquainted; at least two of them had no criminal ties or histories. Studying the hotel registry gives the Op his first breakthrough, uncovering criminal ties and motives in the third victim. In the wild finale, not only does he impersonate a crook; as has been said, Hammett also puts the crook the Op is impersonating on the scene during the Op's impersonation.

This kind of inventiveness brightens the 1924 story, "One Hour." Rather than opening with a dramatic issue, Hammett seizes the reader with a sharp visual image. Vance Richmond's gin-reeking client, Chrostwaite, "a big balloon of a man" with a "round purplish face," is wearing a green plaid suit and a gaudy yellow tie. Because anything he might say would detract from the bold visual image he presents, Hammett makes Richmond his spokesman. A stolen car belonging to Chrostwaite, says Richmond, just killed a local printer. Visiting the print shop, the Op suddenly finds himself outnumbered by four apparent enemies. Hammett builds suspense in the printer's office by slowly explaining both the source and meaning of the danger facing the Op:

> These four men were going to jump me. . . . They were standing stiff-legged and tense, waiting for some move on my part. If I took a step backward—the battle would be on.
> We were close enough for any of the four to have reached out and touched me. One of them I could shoot before I was smothered . . . . That meant that each of them had only one chance out of four of being the victim—low enough odds for any but the most cowardly of men.

The suspense tightens before it snaps. What looks like unexpected help, a seemingly chance visitor to the print shop, darkens the Op's hopes when he smashes the Op from behind. Op fends off his five attackers with decreasing success until he attracts attention from the street by throwing a cuspidor through the office window. The police break up the one-sided fight and hear Op's reasons for suspecting his five foes of murder. Then a policeman calls an ambulance to take Op to the hospital. The sharply segmented action makes the story sound

60

contrived. It isn't. The artificial-looking frame doesn't poke through the action carefully spread over it. What makes the story flow smoothly is Hammett's narrative skill. Besides building suspense, Hammett uses his materials economically, provides a logical solution, and pads the violence by introducing a compassionate policeman, who makes sure Op is treated for his knocks. He also describes Op's fight with the counterfeiters realistically: "My eyes were no good," says the battered Op, and "My hearing was no better than my sight . . . . There wasn't a sound in the world." Rather than inducing pain, his knocks dull his senses; numbness, not distress, is the body's first reaction to a battering.

An equally impressive fight, though much shorter and smaller scale, comes in "Tom, Dick, or Harry" (1925). Though not an early work, the story contains several of the classic crime-puzzle elements common to Hammett's apprenticeship. A San Francisco family is robbed by someone not seen leaving their apartment building. Not only were the elevator, fire escape, and stairs of the building all watched in the minutes following the robbery; the roof of the next building was also beyond jumping or swinging distance. More imponderables follow. Though several people saw the robber at close range, none can identify him; the straitened family's bickering about the size and age of the robber recalls the witnesses' disagreement over the language allegedly spoken by the killer in Poe's "Rue Morgue." Hammett also includes the classic device of the most likely suspect, whose height, build, and age match those of the robber and who has just pawned a ring stolen from the Toplins. Again following classic examples, Op fastens the guilt on the least likely suspect. In a shocking development, he punches the thief's jaw while the thief is still wearing women's clothes and while all the other characters and the reader believe him to be a woman. The fabric of proof the Op then weaves, though tight and sound, never dispels the shock his haymaker sends through the action. It isn't meant to. Hammett wants a richer response than that supplied by the logic-centered crime-puzzle story. A further humanizing touch, and one which imparts a residue of mystery, comes from the broken ending. Though the thief and his cache both come to light, his clothing and weapon remain at large. Rather than smoothing this inconclusiveness, Hammett, who was trying to break from scientific literary detection, welcomes it, weaving more and more contingency into his later work, especially *Glass Key,* and thus sharpening its realism.

61

Around the time of "Tom, Dick, or Harry," Hammett published several other realistic stories using contrast or reversal as structural principles. One of these, "The House on Turk Street" (1924), begins when a gentle old couple ask Op into their old-fashioned home and then chat companionably with him over spiced cookies and tea. Relaxing over his elderly host's cigar, he feels the cold muzzle of a revolver pressing his neck. He has stumbled into a thieves' den. Another surprise follows with the discovery that the cultured British drawl of one of the gunman's helpers belongs to a Chinese. Then the Chinese approaches the rope-bound Op, presumably to kill him. But he uses his knife to cut Op's ropes, not to stab him. Op's helplessness to this point has created one of the best dramatic effects in all Hammett. For most of the way, Op is alone, tied up, and opposed by two or more armed criminals in hostile surroundings. All of his expectations have been overturned. Yet his helplessness opens the lips of his overconfident captors, who, underrating him, give him the information both to deal with them and convict them once he frees himself. The story's exciting sequel, "The Girl with the Silver Eyes" (1924), carries forward the principle of reversal in its design, which balances that of its model. Whereas "Turk Street" observes strict unity of time and setting, "Silver Eyes," loosely draped over a few weeks, spans several settings, both indoors and out-, and covers a wide social spectrum.

The structural contrasts in "Death on Pine Street" (1924), where the police come under rare attack, both build tension and point the solution. The widow of a man whose death Op is investigating is shrill and nervous, and his ex-mistress is passive and dull. Both women heard the shot that killed Bernard Gilmore; then after identifying him, each slipped away, wanting to avoid incrimination. Each love rival feels she was cast off in favor of the other; thus each has a motive for murder as well as the opportunity to have committed it. Each, too, visited the scene of the crime without seeing the other. Neither is guilty, leaving the only other person seen in the area at the time Gilmore's killer.

Though not as symmetrical in design as "Pine Street," "The Gutting of Couffignal" (1925), another story whose structure depends on contrast, provides more excitement. For one thing, the violence is more frightening for exploding in a remote retirement village rather than in the urban inferno. As Auden showed in "The Guilty Vicarage," crime that occurs in peaceful, harmonious surroundings, by contrasting with its smooth background, induces dread: nothing about easeful Couffignal prepares us for the violence that erupts there. Two manservants of the Op's client dies—one white man and one black, one stabbed and one shot to death. Further contrasts follow. The one-man operation mounted by the Op to stop the thieves is improvised. The systematic looting of the islanders, on the other hand, is carefully planned. The thieves destroy both the bridge and the power lines connecting the island to the mainland before attacking the main street with hand grenades and machine guns. Their carefully planned siege and retreat clash, further, with the clamor caused by a racketing thunderstorm. The big storm also helps unify the action, its clamor joining with the electrical outage to seat most of the action in darkness. Because the Op's eyes don't help him much, he must rely on his hearing. The sounds he hears and interprets control the plot. Auditory imagery plays a larger part in "Couffignal" than in any of Hammett's other stories. Moreover, it moves centerstage without giving the impression of straining Hammett's creativity.

Also taking place outside of San Francisco is the group of western tales consisting of "The Man Who Killed Dan Odams" (1924), "Corkscrew" (1925), and "Nightmare Town" (1927). Since "Dan Odams," a revenge story set in Montana, has already been discussed, the two later works can be given their turn now. Corkscrew, Arizona, is as wild as Couffignal is quiet and slow. In fact, its wildness is what sends Op to Corkscrew, to start with. Even though the place provides excellent farm land, farmers have kept away. The puzzled stockholders of the firm that irrigated and developed the area at great cost want the Op to help them realize their investment. Everybody in town resists him. A local minister accuses him of ignoring the town's worst ills—gambling and prostitution. The town's ruffians and crooks resent his meddling in local affairs. And they're not afraid to show their resentment. Absorbing more punishment in "Corkscrew" than in any other single work, Op is thrown three times from a horse and shot three times, as well as being hammered by fists, during his short term of duty as deputy sheriff. The punishment comes from different sources, as the story's title and twisting plot both suggest. While in Corkscrew, Op unearths rackets in both drugs and immigrant-smuggling; he offends some cowpunchers at a nearby ranch and the owner of a gambling and pool hall; he accidentally steps between a man and his ladylove.

Even though these subplots rule out character depth, the action does narrow to a one-on-one clash. The misunderstanding, leading to gunplay, between the Op and his deluded aide fits a classic plot-pattern of cowboy fiction: after cleaning community sinks, the knight and his squire fall out, often over the issue of sex. Besides enriching the plot, their falling-out sharpens the action, adds a surprise, and restores the knight, who never wanted the squire's woman, to mystery. All works out well in this way at the end of "Corkscrew." His exaggerated male honor deludes Milk Rover into believing that the Op and Clio Landes have impugned his bravery. His calling the Op "Chief" right after their shootout marks the renewal of trust and faith. Clio's explanation of what really happened reconciles the quarrelling men and wins back Milk River's love for herself.

The need to leave Op unencumbered at the end of "Corkscrew" forced Hammett to build the story around male camaraderie. Such is not the case in "Nightmare Town." Because Op doesn't appear in this 1927 work, Hammett can feature sexual love. The strong male bond, a staple of the western, dominates only briefly. Of Steve Threefall's new friendship with Ray Kamp, Hammett says, "Not a thousand words had passed between the two men, but they had as surely become brothers-in-arms as if they had tracked a continent together." Kamp's early death ends this bond. The one between Op and Milk River ran deeper and lasted longer because, unlike Threefall, Op had no romantic tie with a women. Thus, in order to keep motives simple in "Nightmare Town," Hammett kills Kamp as soon as he finishes pulling his narrative load. Were Kamp allowed to live, Hammett would have had to pair him with a woman to avoid having him compete with Nova Vallance for Threefall's attention. He did well to remove Kamp when he did. The job of inventing another woman and working her into the plot would have lengthened the story while adding nothing either to the social criticism or the action sequences.

Threefall's romance with Nova begins disastrously, as he nearly kills her with the car he has driven drunkenly into Izzard from the desert. His travels on four continents haven't taught him as much as Nova already knows, as is seen in her not preferring charges against him. His behavior at the outset shown how much he has to learn. Actuated by male bravado, he has crossed the desert with nothing to put in his stomach beside white liquor. He is then jailed as a public nuisance and fined by a local judge for the exact sum he has in his pockets. "You got me into this jam," he tells Nova the first time he sees her after leaving jail. He is wrong. Her not pressing charges against him has kept his jam from thickening. The readiness he needs comes from learning restraint. Specifically, he stops avenging himself on the town he believes to have wronged him. It is tempting to play community scourge in rotten Izzard. Nearly every crime, wrong, or sin thrives, or seem to thrive there, like arson, extortion, insurance fraud, bootlegging, adultery, and parricide. The one green patch on the landscape, a garden fenced by a twining virgin's bower, suggesting innocence, proves deceptive, for it borders the house of a crooked doctor. Threefall escapes this corruption without defeating it. The ability to resist imposing vigilante justice bulks large in the moral system of the loner. Threefall's manner of leaving Izzard suggests moral readiness of this sort. He both enters and leaves Izzard in a car. But whereas he drove into Izzard in a clattering Ford, raising dust and banging into buildings while charging drunkenly down the main street, he leaves as a passenger in a purring British roadster, with Nova at the controls.

That the woman he nearly ran down at the outset now drives him out of the town where the near-accident occurred adds to a pattern of alternation that runs through the story. Benign-looking Dr. MacPhail, owner of the garden-bordered house where Nova lives, turns out to have been crooked all along. Nova's protector, Larry Ormsby, threatens her as soon as he sees that she and Threefall have clicked. Then he reverses field again by letting the lovers use his cream-colored Vauxhall to escape parched, brutal Izzard. Finally, Rymer, referred to near the end as "the only one in town you can trust," has been feigning blindness in order to spy on his neighbors for a bootlegging syndicate. The fatal shootout between him, the villain pretending virtue, and Ormsby, the good bad man, provides the story's last action before the concluding escape sequence.

Two other stories from the mid-1920s that don't work nearly so well as the ones in the western group are "The Nails in Mr. Cayterer" (1926) and "A Man Named Thin" (1962).[9] Marring both stories is their narrator, the prissy, mannered poet-detective, Robin Thin. The long, self-emedded, highly Latinate second sentence of "Nails" will show how poorly the Philo Vance posture suits Hammett's precision plotting:

Now I did not like deception, no matter how mild, but neither did

65

> I like having Papa quarrel with me, and more forcible, if not ac-
> tually greater, than my abhorrence of duplicity was Papa's an-
> tipathy to my poetry, a prejudice which, I may be excused for
> believing, owed much of its vigor to the fact that he had never
> read, so far as I knew, a single line of my work.

The passage also shows why Thin's choleric father calls him "cold-blooded as a tadpole." Thin's pomposity lacks the snap and verve of Hammett's all-out prose. Nolan has summarized his drawbacks as both a character and narrator: "Thin would rather pursue verse than criminals. His first-person narrative is flowery and self-conscious, and in his weakness and affectation Robin Thin remains one of Hammett's least convincing creations."[10]

Point of view is still another reason why Hammett did well to drop him. His splitting the mind of the detective between Thin and his detective-father created technical problems he never solved. In "A Man Named Thin," the son contributes so much to the solution of the crime that he absorbs his father's function and makes him dramatically unnecessary. In "Nails," the son contributes too little, only coming out of the wings at the end to name the culprit. His emergence, rather than smoothing the action, calls attention to its unevenness. The story's defenders might point out that Thin's voice makes him a presence throughout and that its playfulness suits a plot in which nobody is hurt, jailed, or killed, but only frightened. They would be right. But they would also be neglecting Hammett's inability to tune Thin's verbal affectations to the action. Its lack of stylistic control disjoints voice from plot. A story that fights itself, "Nails" is often a fight to read.

A set of later stories whose failure recalls that of the two Thin tales are the Sam Spade adventures, "A Man Called Spade," "Too Many Have Lived," and "They Can Only Hang You Once." As he did in the Thin tales, Hammett wrote these 1932 works against the grain of his creativity. The lure was money. Written to order for *American* and *Colliers,* high-paying slick magazines which published no hard-boiled fiction, staple of the pulps, the stories have little forward drive. Largely accountable for their blandness is Spade himself, who scarcely resembles his splendid 1930 archetype. The glowering, grimacing Spade of *Falcon* has mellowed into a dreamy-eyed reasoner. Esoteric learning rather than street sense wins the day for him in "Too Many," where his knowledge of carnival slang breaks the case and delivers the culprit into his hands.

Though the second half of the 1920s produced the two Robin Thin misfires, it also brought forth some of Hammett's best short stories. The inventiveness of the dialogue, atmosphere, and fight scenes of "Dead Yellow Women" (1925) rivals that of the novels. The page-long biography Hammett invents for an imaginary criminal prefigures similar set pieces in "Knockover" and *The Thin Man*. Then there is the brilliant verbal combat. The dueling rhythm of Op's talks with the Chinatown ganglord, Chang Li Ching, makes us regret that Hammett didn't pit the two men against each other in another story. Such speculation is reasonable. Op and Chang only fight each other verbally and psychologically, hinting, however subtly, that Hammett had thought about matching the two men in physical, perhaps mortal, combat in a later work. Op's admiration for Chang also suggests that Hammett may have wanted to bring him back as a series villain, in the mold of Professor Moriarty or Dr. Fu Manchu: "I liked him. He had humor, brains, nerve, everything. To jam him in a cell would be a trick you'd want to write home about. He was my idea of a man worth working against."

But Hammett has no series villain, Chinese or otherwise. On the contrary, he will disparage rather than romanticize crime, as in another 1925 story, "Ruffian's Wife," where a woman of regular habits discovers her glamorous rover of a husband to be a coward, thief, and killer. Romantic illusions about crime burst in the later stories. The escape of the mastermind of the big bank robbery after betraying his confederates climaxes "Knockover." But his death in "$106,000 Blood Money" enjoys no prominence. It is one of several; it happens quickly; coming midway through the story, it gains no heightening from plot structure. Had Chang Li Ching ever returned to the Hammett canon, his above-mentioned fight-to-the-death would have probably matched him against another criminal, as in "Ruffian's Wife," not the Op. Crime usually defeats itself in Hammett, because of the greed and treachery of criminals; a money belt containing stolen money in "Ruffian's Wife" looks like "an overfed snake." The detective need only play the catalyst, stirring things up between people who distrust and dislike one another to begin with.

The Op's high professional ethics move to the front in "The Main Death" (1927). Hired to investigate a murder, Op won't spy on his client's wife, suspected by the client to have been his business associate's lover. Op's recovery of the money that made the associate

67

murderable shows wit, decisiveness, and compassion. By robbing the robbers, rather than invoking due process, he salvages the reputation of Enid Gungen, which would not have survived a court trial. No God-figure who metes out justice or calms marital strife, he leaves the troubled Gungens to make their own peace, thus placing moral responsibility where it belongs while protecting the reputation of his firm. The end of the story finds the dainty, gaudy art dealer, Bruno Gungen, fuming ineffectually.

A story that conveys a different kind of frustration, at first look, is "Fly Paper" (1929). Though Op reasons brilliantly, moves quickly, and deals effectively with witnesses, he arrests no villain. Leisurely at the start, "Fly Paper" has a logic so rigorous and a design so severe that its ambience is non-literary. A full examination of clues, evidence, and suspects leads inescapably to a verdict of suicide, which Op calls "the only total that what we've got will add up to." Readers looking for a surprising disclosure of some unlikely suspect's guilt may regret this downbeat finale. But what the story loses in drama by bypassing a dazzling plot-twist at the end, it gains in realism. Nor does the realism thin to a dry factual report. Several memorable characters, the favorite motif of the errant daughter of a rich, prominent father, and a challenge that tests both Op's mind and muscle all give the story an integrity that gains from its structural rigor.

Hammett exercises the same technical control on a broader, richer canvas in "This King Business" (1927), but at the cost of making the Op act out of character; the charms of a Balkan beauty make him mix sentiment and detection. It's important to point out that the sentiment is innocent. The inconsistency in Op's character, modulated by the absence of sexual expectation, proved a worthwhile sacrifice; without it, the story would lack much of its grip. Set in Stefania, capital of Muravia, "youngest and smallest of the Balkan states," the story shows Hammett at his most inventive. He invests Muravia with a history, a topography, and a politics. He populates Stefania, gives it a local government and a newwork of streets, and then builds it a train station and a luxury hotel, a police headquarters and an Executive Residence. Balkan ferocity flares out when an officer who flogs one of his men later tumbles into an angry crowd, which dismembers him. The story also describes the eastern European political temper, fusing mass psychology and the psychology of leadership within a Balkan setting. With great self-confidence, a leading contender for the disputed Muravian throne plays on the collective fears and hopes of his agrarian public. To wipe out both partners and rivals, he represents his own greed as theirs. But he acts ignobly for the commonweal. Unlike the petty bureaucrat, the statesman will rate the good of his people above his own welfare. He can't afford high morals. Muravia's short-reigned king does his duty, but turns from the groundling, i.e., the Op, who reminds him of it.

The dynamics of power surge to the fore in the companion stories, "The Big Knockover" and "$106,000 Blood Money." The San Francisco setting of these stories about gang warfare calls for a different technique from that of "This King Business." Like "Corkscrew" before them and *Red Harvest* after them, these 1927 stories grow by accretion rather than internal development. For instance, a character will move to center stage and dominate the action until he's killed. Then somebody else will take his place. This serial, as opposed to organic, structure has a purpose and a theme: Op is fighting crime rather than a specific criminal; richness of detail and narrative speed communicating the reality of his struggle. No single foe occupies him for long. The most spectacular figure in "Knockover," Big Flora Brace, described as "broad-shouldered, deep-bosomed, thick-armed, with a pink throat which for all its smoothness was muscled like a wrestler's," enters a scant quarter of the way from the end. Her queenly reign is even more condensed. Disposed of quickly, she is forgotten in the final stretch. The crime lord who replaces her as the mechanism of the plot is himself stopped in "$106,000 Blood Money" without much ceremony; though the object of a city-wide blood chase, he first appears eight pages from the end and dies two pages later.

Published in 1943 as a 40,000-word novel called *Blood Money,*[11] the stories put forth a terrifying vision of American life. San Francisco looks like "hell . . . on a holiday" when some 150 criminals from all over the United States flood the city to rob its two richest banks. The local police lack both the men and the equipment to stop the caper, during which sixteen policemen and twelve bystanders die. But the knockover of the title of the novel's first part refers to the betrayal of the thieves. No payoff takes place. Rather than paying his aides, old Papadopoulos either strands or kills them. The wholesale double-cross has dangerous by-products. San Francisco now crawls with angry, sold-out criminals looking to raise traveling money for a ticket home. Their scramble for money depicts life under capitalism to the

69

Marxist Hammett, Steven Marcus calling it "the war of each against all, and of all against all."[12] Alliances form and break as prospects of moving closer to the stolen money brighten or dim. Even Op exploits others. He rescues the gangster Red O'Leary from a saloon brawl, then leads him down an (unnecessarily) elaborate network of corridors, back doors and alleys, only to shoot him in the back. Then he takes O'Leary to his friends' den, where the bullet is removed. He has acted with such seeming inconsistency because, believing that O'Leary knows the location of the stolen money, he wants to watch him. Holding no brief with the truism of honor among thieves, O'Leary would sell out his confederates if given the chance. And so would the confederates sell out each other. This deceit is a product of free enterprise, Hammett believes. The system destroys itself by making criminals of all. The relief promised by foreign markets, symbolized by the ability of the heist to bring in thieves from everywhere, never comes. The powerful and the rich are also the most corrupt. Hence, their survival. But because greed begets greed, nobody's survival is assured. As Marcus says, gangsters could easily overrun society. Only their selfishness, which capitalism encourages, blocks a wholesale criminal takeover of America. They don't trust each other enough to organize:

> The only thing that prevents the criminal ascendancy from turning into permanent tyranny is that the crooks who take over society cannot cooperate with one another, repeatedly fall out with each other, and return to the . . . anarchy out of which they have monentarily arisen. In Hammett, society and social relations are dominated by the principle of basic mistrust.[13]

The collapse, or self-fulfillment, of the American way in *Blood Money* includes the breakdown of public institutions, symbolized by the failure of the police to stop the banks from being gutted. Also smirched is the Continental Detective Agency. As in "The Creeping Siamese" (1926), the Agency's involvement in crime goes beyond detection. Ann Newhall, a millionaire's daughter lured and then trapped by crime, has as her opposite number Jack Counihan. "A Handsome op, besides being a fashion plate and a social butterfly and the heir to millions," Jack prefers crime to honest detective work. This rich man's son acts as a deep-cover agent for the robbers and thus discredits the Agency in the same way that Soviet infiltrators like Guy

70

Burgess, Donald Maclean, and Kim Philby smirched British security in the 1950s. Called in to help justice, the Continental only frustrates it so long as Jack is on their payroll. The criminal who perverts justice from within the law is the hardest to detect. He thus poses more danger than other criminals. Though Hammett never says that disillusionment with the prizes won by his father's millions led Counihan to crime, he does convey the havoc caused by criminal infiltration of the law. In-house surveillance becomes the law's chief business. Because operatives can undermine society so disastrously by fronting for criminals, they demand watching. And security demands that the watchers be watched, too. This system defeats its own aims. Besides running up the price of a detective's services, it increases the number of detectives in any given agency to the point where the agency has too much staff to work smoothly. Or perhaps, work at all: overstaffing also creates the disorder and morale problems that the infiltrator secretly loves. The very steps taken to stop him help him.

Blood Money shows the incredibly short hop between hardboiled detective fiction and the cold-war novel of international intrigue. What is more, as the parallel with British security in the 1950s suggests, it also prophesies the dangers of both ignoring and adopting advanced technology in surveillance at all levels.

IV

Philip Durham believes that Hammett's best stories came out between 1927-30. The ones that followed he calls "quite ordinary."[14] He is wrong. He is wrong, too, about the moral decline he notes in Op. Carolyn Wells chose the Op-narrated "Death and Company" as one of the twenty best detective stories of 1930-31. As has been seen, Op tends the bullet-shattered leg of the killer in this, his last adventure. And though he does go "blood-simple" in *Red Harvest,* he exercises patience and tact throughout *The Dain Curse.* Durham also flubs his facts. The "sheer pleasure"[15] Op takes in meting out violence in "Women, Politics, and Murder" doesn't fit Durham's thesis. The story, also called "Death on Pine Street," having come out in 1924, won't support the argument that the Op's behavior declined toward the end; by 1924, he wasn't even mid-career. A later story that shows Op at peak form is "The Farewell Murder" (1930), which later

71

supplied the script for the 1939 film, *Another Thin Man*. Though the title invokes sadness and loss, there's nothing wistful about the action. Horror story rather than documented urban realism, "Farewell" features primitive motives, atrocities, and a vanishing corpse. Most of the shock effects, furthermore, occur in or near an isolated mansion. Accentuating their jolt are the numerous soft tones laving the narrative—one person's gray eyes and sand-colored pajamas, the gray waterproof cap and gray coat worn by a chauffeur, the tan Stutz the chauffeur drives, and the gray, white, and silver appointments of his employer's living room.

The story reflects Hammett's knowledge of the value of contrast for dramatic heightening. It also controls its materials so as to use contrast effectively. At the start, Op is met at the Farewell train station by an impassive, flat-faced man who either won't or can't speak. On the road to the Kavalov mansion, the sight of a man with a knife handle jutting from his chest makes the silent chauffeur shriek in horror. The Op orders the car stopped and walks back to the death-site. No corpse. Nor are there any bloodstains or footprints nearby. Then the chauffeur is gone. The quiet last paragraph of Part One voices our fears while sustaining the mystery generated by what has happened: "It looked, I thought, as if Mr. Kavalov might be right in thinking he needed a detective."

As happened in "The Tenth Clew," the story uses the convention of the old wrong revenged as a red herring. Twelve years ago in Cairo, a British army captain may have been punished for a crime performed by the Op's client, Kavalov. Hammett shapes this legacy from Ibsen's *Pillars of the Community* (1877) and *The Wild Duck* (1885) to the eerie effect he has been building. Captain Sherry has rented a cottage near the Kavalov estate, not to kill his old enemy, he claims, but to witness his death, a vision of which came to him in a dream. Kavalov's servants and farm hands are all scared. His son-in-law's Airedale puppy is found headless, tailless, and gutted, with his remains skewered over an outdoors flame, voodoo style. Then Kavalov is murdered, but at a time when Captain Sherry is out of the district. Sherry's departure, the butchering of the dog, and the corpse at the side of the road in Part One, though, are all smokescreens, cast to hide the trail to the killer, Kavalov's son-in-law and Sherry's accomplice. The work ends on a typical Hammett note; the accomplices turn on each other.

72

Op's problem in "Farewell," like Sherlock Holmes's in "The Speckled Band," is not who, but how. Though some 400 miles away when Kavalov died, Sherry was guilty. He and his accomplice explain the murder-plot during their falling-out over Kavalov's will. But the Op doesn't stand by passively during the recitation. He can't afford to, since he needs hard evidence to convict and hang the guilty son-in-law. Sherry's dying message gives him the necessary evidence. By asking the dead or dying Sherry if his partner killed Kavalov and then nodding Sherry's head for him with hidden fingers, Op tricks the son-in-law into believing that his ex-partner confirmed his guilt. The dying message is one of several literary conventions used in "Farewell." Far from revelling in violence, the story incorporates more elements of classic detective fiction than any other Hammett work. Besides the remote country house setting, there is a medical report, the assembling of the whole household in the living room after the murder, and the questioning of servants, guests, and family. Also hewing to the curve of a plot like that of Agatha Christie's *Mysterious Affair at Styles* (1920) is the pattern of detection. After the official investigators are stumped, the private detective comes in and solves the case. He solves it, moreover, by examining physical evidence—the direction and pressure of the slash in a slit-throat murder.

Lending further conviction to the story is the menu for the sumptuous, multi-course dinner the Op has with the Kavalov family his first night at the mansion. Hammett's most famous catalog remains the one naming the dead crooks in "Knockover." As in Homer, this catalog defines a society and its ethical code by listing carefully selected and arranged biographical data. A sign of its importance in "Knockover," again as in Homer, inheres in Hammett's stopping the action to recite it. The menu in "Farewell" fits more smoothly into the action. Like the Homeric roster in "Knockover," it is a creation-myth, calling into being a whole catalog of details by naming them. As an act of creation, it rivals similar catalogs in Thomas Wolfe, whose *Look Homeward, Angel* (1929) came out a year before "Farewell" and may have been on Hammett's mind during the writing of the story:

> Two men servants waited on us. There was a lot of food and all of it was well turned out. We ate caviar, some sort of consommé, sand dabs, potatoes and cucumber jelly, roast lamb, corn and string beans, asparagus, wild duck and hominy cakes, artichoke-

and-tomato salad, and orange ice. We drank white wine, claret, Burgundy, coffee and *crème de menthe.*

"Woman in the Dark" (1933) also gains from Hammett's vivid sensory imagination. This tale of outcasts and aliens (the hero's name, Brazil, labels him an outsider) contains several original symbols of homelessness. Kane Robson's shooting of Brazil's dog conveys the destruction of both neighborly trust and the traditional bond joining landlord to tenant. Then another man is feared dead when his head strikes a fireplace, emblem of homey cheer. At the end, where Brazil seems to have lost Luise Fischer to Robson, her former patron, she has on a pale negligee and pale slippers in contrast to the defiant red she wore as a fugitive. This color symbolism draws us into Brazil's mind, reproducing his exact visual image of Luise and the gloom it registers. Hammett's delicate handling of the rhythmically orchestrated color symbolism also argues an artistic control that held firm during his prime as a writer. Similar control strengthens the late story, "Nightshade" (1933), whose last-sentence revelation that its narrator is a black man changes the meaning of everything that precedes it. Hammett deserves to stand alongside Fitzgerald and Hemingway as a short-story writer. By coincidence, he also wrote about the same number of short stories as Conan Doyle, whose always popular work has started to crash anthologies used in college courses. Hammett should have the same recognition. The Sherlock Holmes stories have been widely available for years. To give Hammett the same treatment would extend our knowledge of how people acted and felt during one of our most colorful eras. A complete collected edition of his short fiction would also promote greater understanding of his growth, both as social historian and literary artist.

V

But what would the editor of such a collection do about "Tulip" (1966)? The fifty pages that Hammett wrote of his late autobiographical novel reflect little growth or stature. The work's slowness becomes apparent from the start, "Tulip" revealing straightaway what it is not—fast-moving urban realism. The unusually long (sixty-six words) first sentence differs sharply from the tight, muscular phrasing of most of the Op stories. The rural setting is also important. The narrator's attempt to shoot a fox while camped in a roothole summons up Hammett "the woodsman and . . . hunter" who enjoyed "isolated places where there were animals, birds, bugs, and sounds,"[16] as Joseph Blotner spoke of him in *Faulkner, A Biography*. Other aspects of Hammett infuse the fragment, too. The great range of learning Lillian Hellman claimed for him in her introduction to *The Big Knockover* shows in the discussions of math, physics, and Rosicrucian history by Pop, the Hammett character. Autobiography runs strong in "Tulip." Other parallels between Hammett and Pop (the nickname given Hammett by his barracks mates in World War II) include a bout with tuberculosis, a writing career, a tour of military duty in the Aleutians, a recent victory over the bottle, and a still more recent prison term in a federal jail.

The title of the unfinished work-in-progress refers to Pop's friend and former army commander. Pop and Tulip enjoy a rough male comradeship, in which half-serious insults and quarrels play a big part. Pop calls Tulip "a dull and foolish man who goes around doing dull and foolish things," and Tulip, in turn, accuses Pop of child-molesting. Then Pop, the more skillful baiter, dismisses the verbal barbs to a puzzled listener as "a lot of male nonsense." This alleged nonsense both hides and disguises the high value the men put on their friendship. Each needs the other; each may resent the other for reminding him of his shortcomings. Between them, they make up a whole person. Tulip is thick and muscular, Pop, thin and weary; whereas Pop writes, Tulip, a career soldier, is a man of action. Both, now in their late fifties, served in the Aleutians. Early in the action, Tulip makes up a story reworking some of the materials he has just heard in Pop's account of his vacation. Story-telling, in fact, has brought Tulip to Pop. He wants to collaborate with Pop on a story:

> "I'd rather talk to you about your writing. That's what I came for."
> "You didn't. You came here to talk to me about you."
> "Well, it's the same thing in a way."

Pop, the mind half of the mind-body dualism, resists. Presumably, his resistance stops the collaboration from taking place. But other, perhaps more important, things happen instead. And Hammett may have used balance and contrast to point their importance. Just as Pop was sitting in a roothole at the start, Tulip, his double, is immobilized at the end (Hammett wrote the last half-page of the book), recovering from a leg amputation in a Minneapolis hospital. This time, Pop is the unexpected visitor. Why? Accused of trusting too much to reason, has he dug a deeper hole for himself than the one he appeared in at the outset? Or does he climb out of the pit of abstractions Tulip accused him of inhabiting? Does his friendly visit to the hospital signal new growth? Finally, do the two men reverse roles, like so many other doubles, or foils, in recent literature?

We can never answer these questions. But we don't regret it. Although rich in dramatic materials, "Tulip" has no dramatic structure, the following passage typifying its balked, broken action:

> "Remember that crazy major that wanted us to go in for cattle-raising in the Aleutians after the war, said he could fix it . . . to rent us one of the islands cheap?"
> "For God's sake, you didn't do that? With transportation costs the—"
> "No, I just happened to think about it."

As the passage implies, the elements comprising the fragment don't cohere. Elsewhere, Hammett inserts set pieces—a book review Pop wrote in the 1920s, Pop's yarn about his days as a lung patient in a TB hospital, his first meeting with Tulip in Baltimore in 1930. But Pop and Tulip keep these set pieces from interacting. The men are conceived too narrowly; their friendship is overstylized, outdated, and, because of its predictability, trivialized; they don't care enough about the future to give their common story a forward drive. No wonder Hammett stopped writing about them. Unable to generate movement, they probably bored him. Any excitement they prompt belongs to the past. But the excitement fits no pattern and instigates no rhythm. Perhaps "Tulip" could have recovered from its poor start; the printed fragment may only be an early working draft. On the basis of it, though, few will care. Few *need* care. Hammett offers so much pleasure elsewhere that "Tulip" can be savored for its autobiographical insights and dismissed as a work of art.

3

Fresh Mountain Gore

Hammett's first novel sends the much-traveled Op to the raw, dingy mining town of Personville, also called Poisonville and described as "an ugly city of forty thousand people, set in an ugly notch between two ugly mountains that had been all dirtied up by mining." Joe Gores has identified Personville as an amalgam of Boulder, Colorado and the Montana towns of Butte and Anaconda, the latter a copper-mining center.[1] The mountain setting harks to the old west. Hard-drinking, gun-brandishing rowdies people the city; robberies and shootouts are as commonplace as due process is unknown. But instead of riding stallions, local desperadoes roar through town in Black Marias carrying machine guns and homemade bombs. They roar through town this way nearly every day. "The city is sick from the diseases of violence, greed, and capitalist extortion," says Thompson, adding, "the people are shabby and rumpled in appearance, and dull and gray of eye."[2] The Marxist attack on free enterprise noted by Thompson carries through the whole work. Neither life nor soul is saved in *Red Harvest* (1929); nobody lives clean, works at an honest job, or plays fair if he hopes to survive. The criminals who people the action don't harm society; they constitute it. Political bosses and racketeers have already destroyed civil law, replacing it with gambling and bootlegging, graft and paid-off police. Op's victory at the end doesn't affirm community values. Personville hasn't seen these for years. The evil the Op has routed will reinstate itself because the town has nothing either to replace it or keep it at bay. Hammett doesn't describe the interference rushing into the moral vacuum. The wreckage and bloodshed described in the earlier chapters suggest a cyclical pattern of self-destruction. As *Blood Money* showed, its thirst for money and power has made the United States a nation of idolators whose predictability is only rivaled by its greed.

I

Op learns quickly that Personville's name has no basis in reality. The individual's rights are neither prized nor protected in this gloomy, vice-ridden place. Crime is the dynamic life-line joining the residents of Personville; social values all rivet on crime; the mob decides all. The pre-eminence enjoyed by mob rule makes itself felt straightaway. As in "The Tenth Clew" and "A Man Called Spade," the detective's client dies before meeting the man he had hired to protect him. Donald Willsson, a muckraking newspaper publisher, gets shot to death on a dark, lonely street while the Op is waiting for him in his library. The next day gives Op the background of the murder. Several years ago, Willsson's father, Elihu, "the czar of Poisonville," brought thugs to town to break a workers' strike. The thugs hurt Elihu more than they helped him. After taming the striking mine workers, they entrenched themselves in the city, heretofore Elihu's private preserve:

> Old Elihu didn't know his Italian history. He won the strike, but he lost his hold on the city and the state. To beat the miners he had to let his hired thugs run wild. When the fight was over he couldn't get rid of them. . . . They had won his strike for him and they took the city for their spoils.

Unable to drive out the newly empowered hoodlums, Elihu recently turned the job over to his son. He brought Donald to Personville from Paris, where he had been studying journalism, and gave him control of the town's two newspapers, which he used to mount his reform

78

campaigns.

The campaigns proved embarrassing, for much of Donald's civic crusading incriminated his father, and both father and son knew it. Op's visit to sick, old Elihu brings the noisy insistence from Elihu that Donald was murdered by his wife. Has Elihu something to hide? Less impressed by his bluster than by facts, Op doesn't credit the accusation. But before he has a chance to study Elihu's possible motives for murdering his son, another woman replaces Donald's widow at the center of the plot. Op learns, his second day in Personville, that Donald died just after giving a certified check for $5000 to a local woman named Dinah Brand. Dinah, who lives less than a block away from where Donald was felled, becomes Op's next witness. Described as "a soiled dove . . . a de luxe hustler, a big-league gold-digger," Dinah seems to have turned every male head she has wanted to turn in Personville. But she hardly looks or observes the life style of any town siren: The simple gray frame cottage where she lives with stringy, tubercular Don Rolff is patently middle class; her clothes are both unbecoming and unkempt; though only twenty-five or so, she has started to lose her looks, a process hastened by her carelessly applied makeup. Above all, she's totally mercenary and doesn't pretend otherwise. In a community that has shut out the female graces of gentleness and intuition, women outdo men at their own faults. Thus Op, who has asked the right questions while lowering Dinah's guard with drink, deserves credit for prying information out of her without paying.

This information doesn't define her part, if any, in the death of Donald Willsson, whose $5000 check to her was certified, meaning that payment on it couldn't have been stopped. Hoping to find fresh explanations for the certified check at the home of Donald's father, Op comes up against a more dramatic development—the discovery that Elihu has shot a prowler through the head. The development doesn't rattle him. Taking charge of the interview, he agrees to clean up Personville, but only on his own terms. Elihu must give him a free investigative hand and pay a $10,000 retainer to the Continental Detective Agency. The interview displays Op's best bargaining skills. Not only has he observed official protocol; acting quickly, he has also assessed his new assignment politically, psychologically, and morally: "These people you want taken to the cleaners were friends of yours yesterday," he tells Elihu. "Maybe they will be friends again next week. I don't care about that. But I'm not playing politics for you. I'm not hiring out to help you kick them back in line—with the job being called off then. If you want the job done you'll plank down enough money to pay for a complete job."

High-speed action follows talk, as the plot moves to a dawn raid at a bootlegger's warehouse. Accompanying the police, "a shabby, shifty-eyed crew," Op tries to make peace between the contending forces. A salvo of police bullets that bite into the wall alongside him confirms his statement that he's acting alone and gains him admission into the warehouse. Op reorders his loyalties. Even if he *had* been working for Police Chief John Noonan, the bullets Noonan's men fired at him cancelled that compact. Thus he explains to the bootlegger-gambler, Max "Whisper" Thaler, "You're to be knocked off resisting arrest, or trying to make a getaway"; cheerful, handshaking Noonan would rather execute Thaler, Dinah Brand's latest lover, than let him stand trial before a bought judge for Donald Willsson's death. What is more, the chief suspects Thaler of having killed Tim Noonan, his brother, at a lakeside lodge a year ago. But his primitive justice must wait. Thaler escapes the police stakeout easily, bribing some policemen stationed at the back of his warehouse to free him and his friends. Hammett's brief description of their flight, consisting solely of smooth-fitting one-syllable words, registers accuracy and freshness along with the quality of the sensation being recounted: "One of the blond boys drove. He knew what speed was."

The fast car pulls up in Personville's main business district, where Op names Donald Willsson's killer—a young bank clerk named Robert Albury. Recently dropped by Dinah Brand, Albury turned his frustration upon Donald, who had asked him to certify the $5000 check made out to Dinah. Op includes in the fabric of proof he weaves against Albury the fact that Donald was killed by a .32 caliber pistol, the sort favored by banks (inside information like this often enlivens the fiction of ex-detective Hammett). But his naming of the killer, normally the climax of a murder mystery, gives way to a deeper concern—that of getting even. Having been shot at by the local police, Op seeks revenge. The search both exhausts and taints him. Though brilliant and well timed, his exertions in the twenty remaining chapters of this twenty-seven-chapter novel also endanger his job and life. Nobody can afford revenge. Besides, the American city is beyond justice and redemption. Any reformer will come to grief together with his program for civic reform in the urban jungle, regardless of motives. Once the Op starts playing the lone vigilante, he can't stop, remaining in Personville even after settling his private score. His survival at the end depends as much upon luck as upon strength, skill, and sense. Luck helps him in Chapter 8, where Noonan's men fire ten bullets into his hotel room just after he goes there to turn in for the night. His luck—all ten bullets go astray—doesn't teach him prudence. Rejecting the advice to leave town, he vows once again to take on Poisonville.

But how can one man tackle the mob? The way to an answer lies in the mutual distrust and dislike the crooks feel for each other. Op will set Personville's racketeers against each other by aggravating the ill will already dividing them. His instigations allow him to dispense, rather than bring criminals to, justice. His first chance to play justicer comes with the news of a prize fight taking place locally the next night. In order to change the betting odds, he tells people that the underdog, who is secretly backed by Thaler's mob and money, will knock out the favorite in six rounds or less. Then he blackmails the favorite, who, he knows, has agreed to throw the fight, into winning. Op tightens his hold on his man. Some extra prodding at ringside between rounds of the bout convinces the favorite, who is fighting under an alias, that losing will mean being sent back to Philadelphia to stand trial in a murder case. Despite a slow count by the referee, who is also in on the fix, he knocks out the underdog in the next round. As often happens in Hammett, though, he'd have stood a better chance with the law than with the gamblers he has foiled. No sooner is he declared the winner than a knife flashes down into the ring from a balcony and lodges in his neck.

Things go badly, too, for Thaler, who lost heavily on the fight. In Chapter 14, the book's middle chapter, he is arrested as a suspect in the murder of Tim Noonan. But he is freed this same day—thanks to the best use of the convention of the dying message in all Hammett. Tim Noonan's supposed identification of Max "Whisper" Thaler as his assailant doesn't refer to Thaler at all, but to Bob MacSwain, the husband of Tim's recently castoff mistress: "Max didn't kill Noonan's brother. Tim didn't say *Max*. He tried to say *Mac Swain,* and died before he could finish," Op later tells Dinah. Thaler's release from prison, meanwhile prompts the Op to bring in two helpers from San Francisco, big, good-natured Mickey Linehan and the undersized shadow specialist from Canada, Dick Foley. Their job: to help Op drive wedges between the different gangs in town: "If we can smash things up enough—break the combination—they'll have their knives in each other's backs, doing our work for us," Op tells his helpers. But one gang has already mounted its own divide-and-conquer plot, luring a large detail of police to a remote roadhouse while it robs a big downtown bank. That the bank is owned by Op's client, Elihu, that till recently it had employed Robert Albury, Donald's killer, and that Police Chief Noonan helped get his men out of the city—these realities all tighten a high-speed, high-action novel that sometimes threatens to lurch out of control. Further unity of effect comes from an auto chase accompanied by live bullets stitching the country air. This wildness wears down the characters, though. "I can't go through with it," mutters Noonan afterward. "I'm sick of this butchering. I can't stand any more of it."

Op's reminder that Noonan's wish to avenge his brother's death started the butchering leads to one of the book's best scenes, the so-called peace conference of Chapter 19, which all the town's warweary racketeers attend in order to stop the fighting. Op attends with a different goal in mind. He wants to rid Personville of crime, rather than merely lulling it. Thompson has shown how his tactic of "stirring things up" turns the peace conference into a council of war:

> The Op's "peace conference" is at the same time the most perfect example of machiavellian policy in the novel and the most revealing about the Op himself. The conference is a gathering of all the corrupt powers in Personville. . . . All the parties are deceived in one way or another; only the Op knows the truth, and he chooses when to use it and when to distort it.[3]

"I was in a good spot if I played my hand right, and in a terrible one if I didn't," Op remarks inwardly at the conference. The judgment and decisiveness, timing and grip, he displays in the following moments reveal him a brilliant criminal psychologist. By saying things that either embarrass his hearers or make public their betrayals of each other, he sets them at one another's throats. The concentration of gangsters in a single room begets a cancer of crime, as Op had hoped and planned for. He took no great risk. As borne out in George V. Higgins's *Friends of Eddie Coyle* (1972), professional criminals lead slavishly conventional lives; both freedom and originality of choice are nearly unknown in Hammett's underworld.

The chapters following the big meeting at Elihu's mansion reek of cordite. The meeting's first casualty is Noonan, whose offstage death by gunfire comes early in Chapter 20. This death and the others that follow, though serving Op's ends, sicken his heart. Sounding a good deal like Noonan did before the peace conference, he makes us wonder if he will follow Noonan's example by getting shot. The slow tempo of Chapter 20, during which he explains his malaise to Dinah, builds suspense while smoothing the novel's pace:

> This damned burg's getting me. If I don't get away soon I'll be going blood-simple like the natives. There's been what? A dozen and a half murders since I've been here.

*   *   *

> I've arranged a killing or two in my time, when they were necessary. But this is the first time I've ever got the fever. It's this damned burg. You can't go straight here.

His immersion in death goes deeper than he knows. The nervous strain building over the last several days moves him to lace his gin with laudanum, after which he reels into sleep on Dinah's Chesterfield. He wakes up after two fantastic dreams to find Dinah stabbed to death alongside him, the death weapon, an ice pick, in his hand. As the following passage shows, he seems to react neither morally nor emotionally to the death. Dinah could have been a stranger, and he could have been miles away when he heard of her death, rather than waking up in the same room with her corpse:

> She was lying on her back, dead. Her long muscular legs were stretched out toward the kitchen door. There was a run down the front of her right stocking.
> Slowly, gently, as if afraid of awakening her, I let go the ice pick, drew in my arm, and got up.

The passage has puzzled critics, Hammett's verbal irony having opened a big gap between the murder and the way the murder is reported. What must be kept in mind is that the irony serves Op's narration; Op is recounting the action of *Red Harvest,* not Hammett. Op's coolness after the discovery of Dinah's corpse hides a psychological trauma he had alluded to an hour or so before he passed out when he said, "This . . . planning death is not natural to me. It's what the place has done to me." Strong as he is, he hasn't resisted the moral corrosion exuded by Personville. How could he not be jolted by seeing Dinah dead? Her corpse tells him that he hasn't only planned a death, but that he may have also caused one. His degraded self-image having been enforced by his wild dream, he knows himself capable of murder. This knowledge he prefers to keep to himself. He affects nonchalance and buries his fears in the practical details of inspecting the house, removing his fingerprints from surfaces he may have touched, and making sure his clothes are free of bloodstains. The suspicion that he went berserk and killed Dinah forces him to muster as much self-control as he can.

In making him a murder suspect who must use an alias and limit his walking to dark streets, Dinah's death changes the flow of the action. Cawelti has yoked Op's new identity as a fugitive to changes in narrative structure:

> Hammett shifts the narrative focus from the Op as hunter to the Op as hunted. Instead of manipulator of forces and puppet-master of violence, the Op himself becomes a wanted man. . . . Such a shift is necessary to resolve the moral ambiguities of the Op's role. . . . Hammett must somehow pull his hero out of the moral dilemma created by his immersion in violence.[4]

Op's next job is to find a connection. In order to clear himself, he has to connect Dinah's death to four love letters stolen from her apartment the night she died and later found in the pocket of a freshly murdered attorney. To his surprise, the letters came from his client, Elihu Willsson. Donald never had an affaire with Dinah. Op rushes to Elihu's home, even though it is four o'clock in the morning. Elihu's role in his son's death deepens, since the lawyer Elihu hired to recover the letters may have killed Dinah while carrying out his job. Op doesn't want to incriminate the old man, though; having lost a son and a lover inside of a week, Elihu has already suffered enough. But Op doesn't want to let him off too easily, either. Now that all of his rivals have killed each other off, owing to the peace conference, the self-styled old pirate again controls Personville. What Op wants is that he get the governor's help in bringing order to the broken, exhausted city. He wants order badly enough to blackmail for it. If Elihu doesn't reorganize the mayor's office and the police department for a start, Op will publish the letters he wrote Dinah. Elihu sneers at the threat. Nor does Op want any other response in his deepest heart. He has been appealing silently to Elihu's honor and civic pride. In response to Elihu's "Publish them and be damned!" he gives up the letters and starts to leave the room. Elihu responds in kind by ignoring them. Op's silent appeal has worked; Donald's death will take on a meaning and a purpose. In what is perhaps the book's only bright moment, coming, suitably at dawn, the two men realize that they trust each other.

In keeping with the book's costive spirit, this brightness fades, as the action plays itself out in the drabness of a disused warehouse located on the fringe of town. A local thug who has only made two or three brief appearances in the action admits having killed both "Whisper" Thaler and Dinah. Then he dies of gunshot wounds. The meaning of his death? Artistically, Reno Starkey's death makes little impact because of Reno's minor role in the plot; his first appearance, in fact, following his release from jail, could be lifted from the novel without affecting plot or idea, as could his second, where he is but one of many gangsters attending the peace conference. On the other hand, his death augurs well for Personville, since the new town fathers will have one less crook tempting them with bribery and graft. The augury isn't meant to carry much force. Any happy ending imposed on *Red Harvest* would have played the work false, especially its rough, rowdy setting. Both the depravity running through *Red Harvest* and the angry vision behind it rule out happy endings.

II

Op changes more in *Red Harvest* than in any other work. In the early going, he's the complete professional—playing no wild hunches, protecting his firm, and giving away nothing in his exchanges with witnesses and client. With typical caution, he tells Chief Noonan, when asked to name Donald Willsson's killer, "I'm no good at guessing, especially when I haven't the facts." The facts come to him, though, because he knows how and where to dig for them. He also handles people well—Dinah, who gives him free information; Robert

Albury, who supplies the clues Op needs to fasten Donald's murder on him; old Elihu, who thinks enough of him to pay him $10,000 to clean up Personville. A believer in plain talk, Op rejects both Elihu's man talk and his bogus appeal to social conscience:

> "I want a man to clean this pig-sty of a Poisonville for me, to smoke out the rats, little and big. It's a man's job. Are you a man?"
>
> "What's the use of getting poetic about it?" I growled. "If you've got a fairly honest piece of work to be done in my line, and you want to pay a decent price, maybe I'll take it on. But a lot of foolishness about smoking out rats and pig-pens doesn't mean anything to me."

Later, a grifter who comes to his hotel room offering to kill (the already dead) Chief Noonan for money winds up offering Op money to stay quiet. This, he rejects, as he does all bribes, bonuses, and rewards. Nor does he indulge false heroics. Realizing that fighting crime in Personville goes beyond the power of any single crimefighter, he wires home for help. No wonder he is told, after spending less than a week in Personville, "There's no man in Personville that's got a voice big enough to talk you down."

But where Op can resist the temptations posed by easy money and male bravado, he falls prey to revenge. In his zeal to get back at Noonan for trying to kill him, he forgets to report daily to the home office, as required; he violates both company policy and civil law by dabbling in murder; he alienates his two aides from San Francisco, at least one of whom believes him Dinah's murderer. His moral degeneration is already well advanced by Chapter 15, where he says of his firm, "It's right enough for the Agency to have rules and regulations, but when you're out on a job you've got to do it the best way you can. And anybody that brings any ethics to Poisonville is going to get them all rusty. A report is no place for dirty details, anyway." Not content to bend rules, he soon begins breaking them. Thompson likens his contamination to that of the hand which becomes defiled by the pitch it has touched: "The Op has vowed to clean up a community, to act as a scourge, and we approve. Yet to accomplish the job he has had to employ the corrupt means of that world. In so doing, he has become . . . soiled."[5]

The corrupt means he has adopted are those of the traitor. Betrayal is a fact of daily life in *Red Harvest*. No relationship is immune to it; as Op proves, nobody can rise above it. "Every character," says André Gide, "is trying to deceive all the others and . . . the truth slowly becomes visible through a fog of deception."[6] Betrayal comes easily to Op, as do its uses. By making sure that the boxer "Whisper" Thaler has backed will lose, he sells out the sworn enemy of Chief Noonan, his own would-be killer. Then he turns Thaler over to Noonan because he believes Thaler killed Noonan's brother and deserves to be punished. In the next chapter, though, he helps spring Thaler from jail. He never says whether he already knew of Thaler's innocence when he set up his arrest. In a sense, it doesn't matter; justice isn't at stake. Op wants to confuse Personville's underworld, a job which includes rattling the police, but not vindicating a non-existent moral law. In the process of unnerving criminals and crooked cops, though, he also disorients himself. For most of the second half of the novel, he belongs nowhere—serving neither justice nor crime. The moral world of the loner offers little comfort or hope. The purpose he has been working for has become smudged by the means he has adopted; all is drab and annihilating. The Op of *Red Harvest* is sad and weary, haunted and self-alienated; to do his job, he has had to sacrifice both his professional and personal standards. The novel's last paragraph restores him, the self-betrayed, to the Continental, which will expose him to more lying, cheating, stealing, and killing: "I might just as well have saved the labor and sweat I had put into trying to make my reports harmless. They didn't fool the Old Man. He gave me merry hell."

Responsibility to the Continental should have stopped him from playing the footloose justicer of cowboy fiction who cleans up a troubled town. He returns to the city to be savaged by his chief and then sent out on a new case. His restoration to the brotherhood of detectives is costive, indeed. He has lost the trust of his colleagues. Both he and the Old Man know he had done wrong. But to what end? His efforts in Personville, undertaken at great moral cost to himself, have reaped dubious rewards. As the several aliases he uses during the action imply, he has grown less sure both of himself and the values his firm protects. Perhaps he has lost the moral fiber needed to beat back moral contamination. Any sleuth who goes "blood-simple" so quickly may well doubt his mettle. Although not legally guilty, he has accepted moral blame for much of the bloodshed in Personville, especially Dinah's death.

Op's two laudanum dreams, Freudian fusions of memory, invention, and repression, describe the psyche of a man whose options are running out quickly. The dreams mirror each other. One deals with a man, the other with a woman. A chase is featured in each, one extended and one brief, one horizontal, across the land, and one vertical, to the top of a tall building. But whereas the Op searches for the woman in many cities over a long span of time, his pursuit of the man is limited to part of a Sunday morning. Both dreams end badly. Following the man to a high roof, Op loses his balance and falls to the plaza far below, his hand squeezing the man's small head. His search for the veiled woman ends less catastrophically. Worn out by his fruitless quest, he pauses to rest in a hotel lobby. Suddenly the woman comes into the lobby, marches over to him, and begins kissing him while a crowd of onlookers laugh mockingly. Any moral lesson that can be teased out of these two dreams refers more generally to the Op's stay in Personville than to his part, real or imagined, in Dinah's murder. Why bother to destroy your enemy if you destroy yourself in the process? What good is love if it ends in mockery? These questions pervade the dreams, the egg-like head of Op's victim invoking birth as strongly as the veil worn by the woman invokes death. Yet the dreams reject this symbolism while calling it forth; nearness to the widow-like veil makes for a new start, while union with the symbolic egg brings death. Reaching your goals can either embarrass you or kill you dead, the dreams suggest. Getting what you want can be worse than being denied because the prizes you strive for contain hidden dangers. These flare out when least expected; the woman Op has been seeking materializes unbidden, unannounced, and, as it turns out, unwanted. Op will learn that the satisfaction of desire kills desire and, along with it, maims the spirit. Furthermore, the grief that comes from reaching one's goals touches others. Hunter and hunted die together in Op's second dream. Having played the hunter to this point, he will soon take on the role of the hunted. Not accidentally, he wakes up to find a corpse within arm's reach, literally his own arm. Just as Marx insisted that quantitative changes lead to qualitative ones, so does Hammett show dreams edging into and overtaking consciousness.

The two dreams tone down the novel's extroversion, relating, as had been said, psychic and physical reality. They also portray the futility of goal-oriented behavior in our capitalist state, where getting what you want comes less easily than wanting what you get. Finally, they put the Op near the edge psychologically—ironically, just before he must cope with the novel's worst horror, Dinah's death. No wonder both his words and his deeds have a mechanical quality after he wakes up.

Unfortunately, he joins the walking dead for nothing. The vision put forth by *Red Harvest* is darker than that of "Corkscrew" or "Nightmare Town." Unlike Steve Threefall in "Nightmare Town," he loses the girl; as has been seen, he even suspects himself of having killed her. What is more, Poisonville's future is doubtful. Though "developing into a sweet-smelling and thornless bed of roses," it may soon fester into the weedpatch of corruption it was before Op's arrival. For one thing, it has no society or morality, no ordinary peace-loving, workaday middle class, no home life, churches, or schools. Life in Personville is a battlefield of greedy impulses. Sedans speed through the streets at fifty miles an hour, their passengers firing machine guns or hurling home-made bombs. "No better symbol of the end of the frontier is available than Personville," says Robert B. Parker, "a western city, springing up on the prairie in the wake of the mines."[7] To Hammett, the end of the American frontier probably meant the culmination, or self-fulfillment, of life under capitalism. Brutal, cruel, and vicious, Personville could crush stronger souls than the Op. The novel wasn't written to deal the brave detective a defeat, but to show how capitalism maims and mangles the individual and also how unbridled freedom degenerates into chaos and the rule of force. "He was the first . . . to demonstrate the intimate links between organized crime and politics on all levels,"[8] says Jon Tuska of Hammett in *The Detective in Hollywood* (1978). Death is the price exacted for virtue in *Red Harvest*. Perhaps Op did well to go blood-simple; a corrupt life is better than none at all. The book's one virtuous character, Donald Willsson, dies. Even though he wasn't Dinah Brand's lover, the scatter effect of his father's illicit romance with her kills him. As in Dickens, virtue is ineffectual in *Red Harvest;* his father's letters cost Donald much more than the $5000 he pays for them. The letters attest to the contagion of evil, which sometimes infects and even kills the innocent and the unknowing.

The novel's poetic structure denies renewal. Free enterprise kills freedom; nobody is more badgered than Personville's criminal set,

89

where self-reliance knows no bounds. Dawn, the time for fresh starts, fights fresh starts. Sunlight can't probe Personville's sooty cloud cover or scarred mountains. The police raid Thaler's gambling casino in Chapter 6 at dawn; the only brightness flickering over the sullen, overcast morning coming from the flash given off by the firearm blasts. Perhaps the hope associated with Charles Proctor Dawn's last name inspired Elihu to hire Dawn to recover the incriminating love letters. This Dawn serves darkness. After stealing the letters, he darkens his paymaster's hopes by keeping them. Then darkness falls on him permanently when he dies for his treachery. Street names sometimes convey the moral darkness that absorbs and finally crushes lawyer Dawn. Laurel Avenue, where Donald Willsson lives, represents an oasis in a scrubland of racketeers and their rowdies. The civilized values and natural growth its well-tended greenery implies (Donald's home is built inside a hedged grassplot) have no more chance in Personville than their high-minded protector, who dies before he appears in the action.

Another ironic place name is King Street, where Thaler has his office. Thaler is no king. Nobody reigns in Personville; nobody has a clear title to power and honor. When life's prizes are open to all, the ensuing scramble for them makes everyone a potential casualty. The individualist strain in America has dwarfed the individual. The smashing of due process, i.e., the curtailment of liberty in Personville, may have prompted Hammett to set part of the action in Liberty Street. Let Thompson furnish the last moral overview of the town, and to it let us add the fact that the town's most powerful man, Elihu Willsson, is sick and bedridden most of the way. Only once, at the calamitous peace conference, is he seen out of bed. Op does well to turn down his offer to become town sheriff. An effect can have no more reality than its cause. Its richest and most influential citizen a physical wreck, Personville has little chance of a bright, safe future:

> Personville does indeed seem to be a world devoid of values. The only moral spokesman in the novel is Dan Rolff, and he is suggestively diseased and impotent . . . . The only other moral protest is heard from Dick Foley, one of the Op's detective colleagues who quits the job because he suspects the Op has committed murder. But we see this, too, as an impotent protest.[9]

III

Red Harvest has won some enthusiastic praise, W.P. Kenney terming it "a significant step forward in the American detective novel" and Tuska, with the same warmth, calling it "Hammett's profound and compelling novel of universal corruption in America."[10] In view of the novel's rampant violence, this praise seems excessive. There are too many rackets and racketeers. There are too many clashes between them. Too many bullets fly; too many bombs explode; too much blood is spilled (according to William Ruehlmann, twenty-five murders take place in the novel).[11] This brutality is numbing, not exciting. No sooner are characters introduced than they die. Like *Blood Money*, *Red Harvest* moves forward by agglomeration, not internal development. This pattern doesn't suit the book, trivializing the violence growing out of New World energy by failing to link it to characters we care about. *Red Harvest* has more data than its plot can comfortably assimilate. Nobody except Op stays alive long enough to touch our hearts. A bullet speaks more persuasively than words. But the statement it makes is also final and unanswerable.

This substitution of excess for creative energy stems from the Marxist impulse behind *Red Harvest*. The belief that capitalism destroys character and that the creed of rugged individualism destroys individuality might explain the flatness of the people in the book; Hammett's people don't relate to each other, but to the dynamics of local mob rule. Sincere political sermonizing, though, doesn't always produce good art, especially in the novel, with its traditional commitment to individuality. Politics can't explain the worries caused by the book's first-person narration. A built-in drawback of a work like *Red Harvest* is that its narrator-sleuth sometimes seems to be holding back important information in order to divulge it when his author wants it divulged. Because Op reasons often in *Red Harvest*—naming the murderers of Donald Willsson and Tim Noonan, for instance—he leaves us behind. Only after solving these murders does he confide in us. And with good reason: to have done so beforehand would have spoiled the dramatic effect gained by his revelations. There's no solution to this technical problem other than noting that it doesn't undermine Hammett's sense of fair play: Op has seen and heard no more than the reader has when he names the two murderers. But he works alone; his voice controls the action; this voice, which also controls our responses, doesn't always chime with his thoughts.

What we do hear, though, shows rare technical control, based on Hammett's refusal to give Op privileged information he can use to solve the book's first two murders. Unity both of tone and effect comes from the greed that drives all the characters—greed for power, money, and, in the Op's case, revenge. Its episodic structure doesn't disjoint the novel, Hammett controlling the rhythm of shifting loyalties as treaties form and break in Personville's criminal set. As has been seen, even Op gets drawn into the maneuvering and becomes stained by it. Hammett makes us question the depth of this stain. Does guilty self-knowledge keep the Op from staying in Personville as sheriff? Does he suspect that his moral taint will stop him from serving effectively? Perhaps Personville deserves a sheriff with more moral stamina and self-confidence. Though its citizens have little depth, they span a broad range. Hardly anybody is exhausted by his criminal impulses. Personal motives will sometimes crowd out political or financial ones, causing a good deal of inward suffering. To make Personville more realistic, Hammett includes several sorts of family relationships. Tim Noonan was having an affaire with the wife of Bob MacSwain, his murderer. Now the police chief wants to punish his brother's killer. Elihu Willsson claims his daughter-in-law killed Donald, whose death had nothing to do with his civic reforming or his father's roughneck politics. Finally, Dinah Brand's live-in relationship with her ward, or housemate, the tubercular Dan Rolff, refers in no way to the scramble for money and power.

The enriched portrayal of human purpose created by these personal motives gains firmness from narrative structure. Hammett needs his large cast of criminal characters to convey the pervasiveness of the crime that has gripped Personville and, by extension, America. Yet he also uses the family to fend off narrative sprawl. Thus Donald's secretary is the daughter of Elihu's secretary, and Robert Albury's sister moves to Hurricane Street to watch Dinah after Robert admits having murdered Donald. Further tightening of the plot comes from Hammett's treatment of the numerous deaths. Though not restrained, *Red Harvest* could spatter the reader with more blood than it does. Given the premise that our national heritage rests on violence, the novel's gunplay and bomb-throwing can't offend anybody. But it would have raised hackles if many of the important murders—Donald's, Noonan's, Dinah's, Rolff's, and

Thaler's—didn't take place out of view. No culture can be portrayed artistically if its values aren't dramatized. In *Red Harvest,* Hammett describes the pioneer creed of the right to bear arms while merely reporting the death-by-arms of his main characters. The book is violent but not spectacular or cheap.

If Hammett's good judgment doesn't redeem the novel, it nonetheless sets forth the problems faced in portraying a violent society. *Red Harvest* would be false and dishonest without its clamor, frenzied movement, and murders; Hammett barrages us with images of brutality to convey the mad, wild sensation of American city life during Prohibition. His ability to distance the brutality betokens the control and moral balance that divides art from harangue.

4

The Voice-and-Vision Flimflam

The Dain Curse (1929) softens the relationship between individuals and society from that put forth by the brawling *Red Harvest.* Less tied to social issues, the Hammett of *Dain Curse* is no highminded prosecuting attorney or social philosopher. The moral wilderness of Poisonville gives way to civilization, or what passes for it in the San Francisco of 1929. Ampler and more thoughtful than its roughneck predecessor, *Dain Curse* also moves slower and spills less blood (containing a mere twelve murders to the twenty-five of *Red Harvest*). In place of Marxist melodrama, it offers a Gothic extravagance, a sealed room puzzle of sorts, and the related jobs of curing a young widow of morphine addiction while demythologizing a family curse. These challenges both extend and deepen the novel's tone. *Dain Curse* begins with clarity and hardness of line—the image of a diamond sparkling against the shaggy green background of a lawn. Then it veers into a psychological fog belt created by both the horrors of the family curse and a bogus religious cult set up to fleece its followers. The Op has recovered sufficiently from the ravages of Poisonville to take charge of the varied action. *Dain Curse* makes a notable advance from *Red Harvest.* Although the favorite of few of Hammett's readers, it contains some exciting scenes, covers a range of character types, and, for most of the way, offers tight, smooth plotting.

I

The supposed theft of diamonds valued at about $1000 takes the Op

94

to the San Francisco home of inventor Edgar Leggett. Like the inventors in the first Op story, "Arson Plus" (1923), and *The Thin Man,* the reclusive Leggett exudes mystery. A local jeweler had given him some small, off-color stones, hoping that he could improve their tint with a process he had successfully applied to glass. These hopes come to nothing. Despite a month's hard work, Leggett's secret process failed to remove the brown and yellow stains. His failure makes the theft of the stones puzzling. Why would a thief want jewels that are small, discolored, and not particularly valuable? Op senses something odd in the execution of the theft, too. The thief knew exactly where the jewels were kept, went straight for them, and took nothing else belonging to the Leggetts. He or she made no hurried getaway, either. The jewel on the lawn, Op reasons, was probably planted there to deflect suspicion from the inhabitants of the house, one of whom is the thief. Op's search for the thief produces stories about a prowler seen on the Leggetts' street the nights of and leading up to the robbery. The witnesses' conflicting descriptions of the prowler add suspense and intrigue, as in Poe's "Murders in the Rue Morgue," where every witness within hearing claims the killer to have spoken a different language. The confusion in *Dain Curse* doesn't stem from a nonhuman killer but from the fact that there were two prowlers, one of whom is identified by the Leggetts in the Golden Gate Avenue apartment where he lies murdered, the envelopes that once held the stolen jewels nearby.

Both to bring in an important character and to supply some important insights, Op next rehearses the details of the case with novelist Owen Fitzstephan, whom he had known in New York City five years before. Not only did Fitzstephan's knowledge of the occult help Op catch a crook in New York; his friendship with both Edgar Leggett and the jeweler whose diamonds were stolen from Leggett also makes him a good source of information in the current crime. But more is involved in the relationship between Op and Fitzstephan than crime-stopping. As has been said, the relationship fuses two key impulses in Hammett—those of the detective and the fiction-writer. The fusion asserts itself both physically and temperamentally. In contrast to the pudgy Op's actionism, tall, thin Fitzstephan favors ease and repose. When he works at all, on his books, he works alone; Op, on the other hand, serves a large organization, and he often uses helpers. Balancing

95

Op's commitment to facts, Fitzstephan specializes in the imagined, the remote, and the arcane: "Fitzstephan . . . pretended to be lazier than he was . . . and had a lot of what seemed to be accurate information and original ideas on any subject . . . as long as it was a little out of the ordinary." The chapter in which Fitzstephan is introduced balances nicely. From the stylish Nob Hill flat of Fitzstephan, Op goes to the milling, earthy ghetto where the Leggetts' black maid, Minnie Hershey, lives with her gambler-lover. What interests Op most about his visit to Minnie is the sight of twenty-year-old Gabrielle Leggett leaving Minnie's apartment building. By the next morning, Gabrielle is missing, and neither of her parents will discuss her disappearance. The next chapter, called "Gabrielle," begins by identifying the corpse of Chapter Two (whom Gabrielle had seen) as that of a former New York detective who lost his license and went to jail for bribing jurors in a murder trial.

The events of the chapter both grieve and gladden Op. Though he doesn't learn Louis Upton's role in the jewel theft, he does trace Gabrielle to a well-financed religious cult called the Temple of the Holy Grail, which occupies a six-story apartment building in a good residential neighborhood. Op meets one of the cult's leaders, tall, graceful Aaronia Haldorn, who tells him, in a musical voice, that Gabrielle is sick and doesn't want any visitors. Pointing out that Gabrielle witnessed a robbery and perhaps a murder, as well, he talks his way into her room. Aaronia judged well to call Gabrielle sick. Dazed and twitching from narcotics, she needs to be helped out of the Temple by the Op and her worried, fumbling fiancé, ex-Ivy leaguer, Eric Collinson. One high drama follows another, giving the book power, speed, and surprise. The usual sleepiness gone from his eyes, Fitzstephan announces that Gabrielle's father has killed himself. What follows these startling words is Leggett's suicide letter, the European and South American content of which lends resonance to the crisp, varied action.

Leggett identifies himself at the start of the letter as the French-born, English-educated Maurice Pierre de Mayenne. In 1908, at age twenty-five, he married Lily Dain, daughter of a deceased British naval officer, and had a daughter with her the next year. The early years of the marriage brought trouble. Perhaps even before Gabrielle's birth, Leggett suspected that he didn't love Lily but her sister, Alice. Lily's refusal to give him a divorce so he could marry

Alice angered him so much that he murdered Lily. The murder gained him nothing. He was remanded to Paris from London, where he had taken Alice, convicted, and sentenced to life imprisonment on Devil's Island. Five years later, he escaped to Venezuela, where he found work with a British copper firm. One of his co-workers, though, discovered his identity as an escaped prisoner and threatened to disclose it unless he helped him rob the firm. To avoid being arrested and returned to Devil's Island, de Mayenne had to go along with the robbery. He didn't cooperate any longer than he had to, though, fleeing the country soon thereafter. But his blackmailer found him in Mexico City two months later. The two men fought, and the blackmailer was killed. De Mayenne then fled immediately to the United States. Since 1923, i.e., for the past six years, he had been living in San Francisco under his new name with Alice and Gabrielle, whom he sent for soon after moving to the Bay area.

One spectacular disclosure leads to another in the tightening narrative, Hammett holding the novel's new temporal and spatial spread in close check. The discovery of $15,000 in Leggett's pocket brings the announcement, from Op, that Leggett didn't commit suicide but was murdered. His reasoning relies more on psychological insight and common sense than on material clues:

> He had this money in his pocket. He was going away. He wrote that letter to the police to clear his wife and daughter, so they wouldn't be punished for complicity in his crimes. Did it . . . sound to you like the dying statement of a man who was leaving a wife and daughter he loved? No message, no word, to them—all to the police.

In the sort of demonstration usually saved for the last chapter of a murder mystery, Op fastens the murders of both the dead man and his first wife, Lily, upon Alice. The accusation brings still another surprise. Refusing to cower, Alice, her eyes burning, names Gabrielle her own mother's killer. As in the late novels of Ross Macdonald, *Dain Curse* introduces a childhood trauma that blackens the psyche of an innocent person. The passions giving rise to the trauma unleash primitive force. Leggett had slept with both Dain sisters. Even after marrying Lily, who had started Gabrielle in order to trap him, he continued as Alice's lover. Alice wanted more. With snarling glee, she explains how she taught five-year-old Gabrielle to squeeze the trigger of an unloaded pistol while pointing the pistol at the head of her sleeping mother. Then one day she handed Gabrielle a loaded pistol. Coming home earlier than expected this same day, a stunned Leggett saw the shooting take place. In order to wipe away Gabrielle's memory of killing her mother, he quickly agreed to marry Alice. But Alice will protect Gabrielle no longer. Gloating and chanting, her savagery magnetizing her listeners, she pronounces Gabrielle the inheritrix of the Dain family curse. Her malice is short-lived. Attempting to run away, she dies from bullet wounds while fighting off two would-be captors.

The exposure and punishment of the culprit doesn't end *Dain Curse*. As the novel's title suggests, Hammett must either defuse the curse or deal with its effects on its supposed latest victim, Gabrielle. The curse can't be dismissed as soon as it is introduced, though. Instead, Hammett uses it to bolster the plot. From the Leggetts' lawyer, gaunt, sixtyish Madison Andrews, Op learns that her doctor has consented to Gabrielle's going back to the Temple of the Holy Grail. But now Dr. Riese questions the wisdom of his decision. After thriving for four days at the Temple, Gabrielle seems dazed and shocked. Would her spirits improve at home? She says no. Lawyer Andrews agrees with her fiancé, Eric Collinson, that she may stay at the Haldorns providing that Op take a room near hers and act as an informal bodyguard. What happens his first night at the Temple justifies his presence there. First, Dr. Riese fails to show up for a conference with Op; Minnie Hershey then buys Gabrielle some morphine; later, the stale, lulling odor of dead flowers awakens Op in the middle of the night. Reacting quickly, he finds Gabrielle gone from her room. Along with Eric Collinson, who has come to the Temple looking for the missing Dr. Riese, Op searches for Gabrielle. Their search ends spectacularly, Gabrielle materializing with a bloody dagger and asking to be sentenced to death. Her wild looks and words gain plausibility when she leads the men to the corpse of Dr. Riese, sprawled on the six-story cathedral room's white crystal and silver altar. Gothic menace pervades this part of the action. After taking Gabrielle to her room and leaving her there in Eric's custody, Op goes back to the cathedral room. But he finds nothing to investigate. Dr. Riese's body has been removed.

The next chapter maintains the mystery. In some of his best running prose, Hammett describes Op's fight with a damp, glistening blob that keeps breaking up and remaking itself after appearing in Op's room. Biting, punching, and gouging his ectoplasmic foe, Op wonders if he is drugged or dreaming. (Only later does he learn that the substanceless shape he fought, consisting of light and gas, was piped into his room together with the mind-dulling stale flower scent he smelled before.) Speculation doesn't occupy him for long. Op is given no rest in Chapter 11. After fighting an immaterial enemy in the dark, he battles a real one, from whom he takes the dagger used to kill Dr. Riese. Then he learns that Gabrielle has bolted again, wanting to save Eric from the curse she believes herself to have inherited. But there is no time to look for her, Hammett having crammed this part of the novel with one crisis after another, lest we catch our breath long enough to register disbelief. The chapter's most lurid moment and dramatic climax demands immediate attention. To crown some gruesome, sadistic rite, Joseph Haldorn, leader of the Grail cult, has placed the rope-bound body of his wife, Aaronia, on the same altar where Dr. Riese's corpse lay earlier. Believing himself a stern, unyielding god endowed with the power to take away life, the mystically transformed Joseph wants to kill Aaronia. His divine possession runs so deep that it lets him take seven bullets in his face and body at point blank range without wincing. In the book's bloodiest encounter, Op drives a knife into Joseph's throat and then faints from the strain, physically and psychically worn out.

Like Personville's police force in *Red Harvest,* the Temple of the Holy Grail perverts its avowed mission of protecting people in favor of exploiting them. Its large following among San Francisco's elite lets Hammett criticize both social institutions and trends in organized religion in one stroke. This criticism takes the form of Gothic romance. Now Hammett had used Gothic materials as early as 1923 in "When Luck's Running Good." The six years between "Luck" and *Dain Curse* reveal a new maturity in the handling of Gothic conventions. The religious coloring that seeps through Part Two of *Dain Curse* hearkens back to the convents and monasteries used by Gothic writers 250 years earlier. The corpse that slides in and out of view, the dark corridors, staircases, and rooms, the strange noises, and the unworldly apparition of the mechanical ghost Op fights in Chapter 11 refer just as pointedly to Gothic romance. Like an Anne Radcliffe or a "Monk" Lewis novel, *Dain Curse* asks us to suspend rational disbelief in order to savor the marvelous. The noncognitive supplies the groundwork of Part Two of *Dain Curse*. The villain's madness both creates and controls the suspense; there's no telling what he'll do next. The only certainty is the identity of his victim—Gabrielle. The struggle in a Gothic fiction doesn't pit the villain against the hero, but against the passive heroine. What worries the heroine most is her inability to know the villain's next move, since she can't cope with the unforeseeable. In *Dain Curse,* she doesn't even know the villain's identity. He is only known by his gruesome work—the terrors unleashed at the Temple.

These terrors, though, belong to the Temple at this point. Because nature can offset their harm, Gabrielle leaves the city straightaway in Part Three. Her choice of the fresh, the open, and the unpeopled again comes from Gothic fictional convention. The high-strung heroines of Gothic novels would flinch at the faintest stimulus—an autumn leaf rasping the floor of a stone courtyard or a distantly creaking door. Her drug addiction, the overhanging threat of the Dain curse, and the recent deaths of her doctor, her father, and her stepmother all make Gabrielle as hypersensitive as Emily St. Aubert in Radcliffe's *Mysteries of Udolpho* and, also, just as delusion-prone. Thus she remains the novel's emergency, the focus of the other characters' efforts, and the source of most of the novel's ideas—all while remaining passive, a potential victim. Whatever energies she does display consist of running away, and she usually has somebody with her to work out most of the practical details.

II

Not until Chapter 12, "The Unholy Grail," are the deeds of the Haldorn cult secularized and tamed. Like Part One, Part Two of *Dain Curse* ends with a discussion between Op and his confidante-aide, Owen Fitzstephan, in which the elements of the case are sifted and analyzed for the reader's sake. Joseph Haldorn, Op explains, was an actor who gave up the stage for the pulpit and, living in an age of popular preachers, brought his cult to San Francisco. With him came his wife and his stage mechanic, ex-illusionist Tom Fink, whose ghostly apparitions of illuminated steam gulled the cult's followers. Joseph's godlike transports were also manufactured—out of hypnotic trances first brought on by his wife and later self-induced. Aaronia had to die because she knew that Joseph had fallen in love with Gabrielle and

100

planned to use the girl's guilt to win her heart along with her purse. Coming at the end of the book's second installment in *Black Mask,* Op's disclosures create a provisional ending. Wickedness has come to light, those guilty of it have been punished, reasons have been given, and, finally, the curse has gone away, a sign of which is the marriage of Gabrielle and Eric Collinson. Yet, it comes out early in the next chapter, problems remain. The marriage has fostered more gloom than joy. Marrying so soon after her parents' death, the drugged, nerve-raked girl wasn't capable of acting responsibly. What is more, her selfish fiancé, seizing upon her weakness, married her in Nevada rather than California, to escape the three-day waiting period. His selfishness backfired. The opening words of Part Three of *Dain Curse,* "Queseda," dispel any gladness caused by the routing of the cultists. In a wire sent from Queseda, a coastal resort town some eighty miles south of San Francisco, a fretful Eric sends for the Op. His worries were perhaps more urgent than he knew, for the next chapter shows Op dragging his corpse from the ocean later that evening.

Torn shrubbery nearby convinces Op that Eric was pushed off a nearby cliff. But who pushed him? Along with the novel's new setting comes a new set of characters and an expanded roster of suspects. From one local woman, Op learns that Grabrielle wouldn't let Eric sleep with her (a report later confirmed by Gabrielle, who claims she is still a virgin). The woman, the deputy, the sheriff, the coroner, and the D.A. all believe her guilty of murdering Eric, as do Eric's lumber baron father and brother, who have come down from San Francisco. Only Op suspends judgment. In the meantime, Gabrielle, the most likely suspect, is missing again. Nor do the sexual and professional rivalries of the Queseda set bring Op closer to her till a letter written by the town marshal's wife before she was choked to death sends the men to a bootlegger's cave. Here, a much-weakened Gabrielle turns up with the marshal's wife's ex-lover. Any information the burly ex-lover could give about the deaths of Eric and Daisy Cotton vanishes in a gunfight he foolishly starts after finding himself trapped by the police.

Now Harvey Whidden's death in Chapter 17 creates an unexpected textual problem besides deepening the novel's intrigue. The fourth and last *Black Mask* installment (February 1929) begins with Chapter 18, "The Pineapple," which opens some hours after Whidden's death. The four-part division is apt. Besides spreading the action evenly,

Part Four also helps organize it. With Chapter 18, the search for Gabrielle ends and her rehabilitation begins. A coherent unit, Part Four also brings the action full circle to San Francisco, deals with the alleged curse, and, with a crash at the outset, introduces one last mystery whose unravelling leads to the book's solution.

The internal structure of the four parts reflects the demands of the changing plot. Parts One and Two ended with an intellectual, verbally achieved, climax; Op and Fitzstephan were reviewing the case. To provide contrast, to speed the action, and to introduce another death, the magazine version of Part Three ended with the gunfight near the bootlegger's cave. Yet all isn't sacrificed to plotting. Gabrielle's rescue party at the cave included Fitzstephan and Op, and the two men are together again at the start of Chapter 18. The opening sentence of the novel's last chapter (Chapter 23), furthermore, "Owen Fitzstephan never spoke to me again," completes the process Hammett hinted at near the end of Part Three by breaking his pattern of ending each part of the action with a confidential talk between Op and Fitzstephan. The need for this discussion of narrative design? Either Hammett forgot to indicate that Chapter 18 begins a new section of the novel, as he did at the start of Chapters 1, 9, and 13, or the printer forgot to post the section title and Hammett never caught his omission while reading proof. The error came easily enough, since the titles of the first three parts differ from those used in *Black Mask*. Yet it also distorts the plot; the action splits much more smoothly and makes more sense with a break at the end of Chapter 17 than in its present, lopsided three-part format. Besides, Part Three, with its clockwork characters, is the least successful part of the novel. The reader is glad it's over. The announcement of a new section beginning with Chapter 18, where the action peaks, would reassure him in his gladness.

One of the novel's best surprises also comes in Chapter 18. While the two men are talking, Tom Fink, special-effects engineer at the Holy Grail, enters the room. A minute later, a bomb, or pineapple, explodes. The roaring, juddering room seems to have been ripped out of reality. Part of this crashing impact comes from Hammett's description of it. Like Op, we are jolted by the explosion before we know what has happened. Rather than saying that a bomb has gone off, Hammett recreates the blast's overwhelming physical suddenness: "The door to my room split open. Floors, walls, and ceilings wriggled under, around, and over us. There was too much noise to be heard—a roar that was felt bodily." The person hurt most by the blast is Owen Fitzstephan, with an arm, most of a leg, and the side of his face blown off and his body twisted and torn. As soon as he is taken to a hospital, where he expected to die forthwith, Op begins pondering the problem of how the bomb got into the room.

But his thoughts turn quickly. He must help tormented Gabrielle forgive and accept herself. Strengthening him is his belief in a different heredity from that plaguing Gabrielle. Arguing that she has inherited the toughness and moral stamina of her father rather than her aunt-stepmother's madness, he tells her that she's normal. What is more, he'll confirm her normality by helping overcome her morphine habit. The effort calls for a deft double remove. In order to hearten Gabrielle, he pretends to be pretending that he hasn't fallen in love with her. The maneuver works. Feeling loved by a person of worth gives her the self-confidence to resist drugs. So impressed is she with Op that she asks him, "Do I believe in you because you're sincere? Or because you've learned how—as a trick of your business—to make people believe in you?" Her later actions show her to have fallen into something greater than a belief. She calls Op "the nicest man in the world," looks for ways to be with him, and tries to tempt him by parading in front of him with her robe open. His exchanges with her during her cure comprise a psychological shadow game whose timing, delicacy, and tenderness have not been sufficiently credited. Only after settling her into a seaside hideaway with a housekeeper-companion and seeing her through her worst withdrawal seizures does he begin investigating the bomb-blast.

Convinced that the bomb entered the room with engineer-magician Tom Fink, he goes to Fitzstephan's hospital room; miraculously, the novelist is going to survive. But Op doesn't congratulate him. Instead, he charges Fitzstephan with setting off the bomb, with arranging Dr. Riese's murder, and with killing Eric Collinson. These accusations rock the reader, even though Op had unleashed similar ones, bypassing logical preambles, from the first story featuring him, "Arson Plus" (1923), to *Red Harvest*. If he acts sadistically by confronting the killer with his guilt while the killer lies helpless, "ninety percent bandages," his anger toward Fitzstephan runs deep. Fitzstephan has caused Gabrielle's worst troubles—her morphine habit, her believing herself the carrier of a curse, her being widowed. Op's assault doesn't make Fitzstephan flinch. He unloads heavy fire of his own by revealing

103

himself a Dain and then, in a shocking reversal of conventional justice, announcing that his many crimes will acquit rather than convict him:

> I shall insist on the curse, shall use it to save my dear neck . . . .
> You're going to see a most remarkable defense, a circus . . . .The
> number of my own crimes will be to my advantage, on the theory
> that nobody but a lunatic could have committed so many. And
> won't they be many? I'll produce crimes and crimes, dating from
> the cradle.

Op counters with a surprise of his own—agreeing coolly that Fitzstephan probably won't be convicted. But he also stops Fitzstephan from enjoying his freedom by arguing that his insanity plea will rest on fact rather than expediency. This argument rattles Fitzstephan, who courts madness, but only as a cover or pretence. Op interprets the courtship differently. Denying his friend the satisfaction of breaking the law and getting away with it gives him the edge in the obscure psychological duel. His testifying in court that Fitzstephan's physical injuries entitle him to escape hanging also reveals him a nimble, if not original, moralist. Like the judge in "The Judge Laughed Last" (1924), Op has risen above the law to vindicate the law. Fitzstephan's acquittal glorifies the Op. He has outpaced his foil as an artist, blurring the frontier between imagination and reality. If Fitzstephan had rejected his fiction, he'd have gone on talking to him. His silence confirms the superiority of Op's creativity.

Everything tallies. In the last chapter, Op tells how Fitzstephan murdered both Alice Dain and Edgar Leggett in addition to Daisy Cotton, Dr. Riese, and Eric Collinson. What matters most about these disclosures is that they lift all moral blame from Gabrielle. She can laugh at the Dain curse. If the curse does survive, its host is Fitzstephan, who is safely out of her way on an island in remote Puget Sound. Having lived at a great moral distance from his kind, he now inhabits a geographical wilderness, too. This marginal existence ties in with *Black Mask* aesthetics. The cynical outlook put forth by the magazine's editorial policy ruled out happy endings; the urban barrens are no place for triumph or affirmation. Fitzstephan will be nursed by Aaronia Haldorn, an adultress, swindler, and possible madwoman. Yet she cares enough for him to nurse him. Depravity hasn't overtaken all, Hammett scattering over his ravaged world some grains of tenderness.

104

III

Although Hammett probably intended no thematic tie between the two novels, the Op of *Dain Curse* outshines the weary, morally tainted detective of *Red Harvest*. His recovery deserves comment, for he may still be reeling from his Personville assignment. His quickly changing the subject when Personville is mentioned in the later book betokens both new control and strength. Bent and stooped while searching the Leggetts' lawn for diamonds at the outset, he speaks of inspecting the lawn closely but "without going it on all fours." This hunched-over figure attains full moral and professional growth as the action unfolds. Op impresses us throughout. He both recognizes the symptoms of and knows how to treat morphine addiction. (This expertise makes us ask why the physician Dr. Riese presumably overlooked Gabrielle's addiction, at least until her fifth day at the Temple, when his overdue diagnosis probably caused his death.) Besides saving Gabrielle, he also unriddles the curse while both outwitting and punishing the murderer. How does he succeed so well? The Op of *Dain Curse* has more refined ideas about right and wrong, guilt and punishment, than those reflected in the retributive morality of his profession. Acting with compassion and strength, he stops Aaronia Haldorn from seeing Gabrielle during the latter's convalescence; no good can come from a meeting between Aaronia and the woman she believes stole her husband's heart. Even after Aaronia, angry at being turned away, tries to shoot Op, he won't try to convict her for her part in the cult swindle. Protecting Gabrielle comes first with him. Rather than punishing the guilty Aaronia, he helps Gabrielle regain hope and self-esteem. This job he does with great dedication and insight. His always referring to her to the others as "Mrs. Collinson" denotes the respect he wants given her during her ordeal.

For the ordeal, she needs whatever boosts she can get. As usual, Op comes through splendidly. Just as he convinces Fitzstephan of his madness, he confirms Gabrielle's sanity and worth. He does this in different ways, flirting with her, complimenting her, and scolding her. He holds her down during her seizures; he sleeps in a chair in her room. All this inspires her. The trouble he goes to reflects a faith that gives her faith in herself. Nothing clouds the moral clarity of his conduct with her. Though the others try to spare her the pain of seeing her dead father and hearing his alleged suicide letter, Op overrules them.

105

She has every right to see her father and hear his last words. Moreover, she can handle the ordeal. Aware of her hypersensitivity, Op probably thought that seeing her father's corpse first hand would haunt Gabrielle less than fantasizing about it. He may have been right; rarely, if ever, does Gabrielle mention her father after seeing him dead.

Op's foil, Owen Fitzstephan, supplies an intellectual and analytical thrust missing from *Red Harvest*. His novelist's curiosity about motives helps him interpret the novel for us psychologically, making him a quasi-Watson. But the second mind he brings to the novel is sick and twisted. Eccentric sleuths like Dupin and Holmes, Poirot and Nero Wolfe, had sober, ordinary chroniclers. In *Dain Curse,* the sleuth is sober and ordinary. Thus, to avoid any overlapping of dramatic roles, his Watson must be eccentric. Hammett legitimizes Fitzstephan's involvement with the Temple swindle by spiriting him out of the mainstream of life. Fitzstephan likes lurid tones and exotic effects, a degenerate Tom Sawyer. When the literal-minded Op dismisses the Dain curse as "words in an angry woman's mouth," Fitzstephan accuses him of draining life's color. This preference for the obscure over the ordinary also turns his friendship with Op into a conflict between criminal and crime-stopper. Underlying his zest for strange vibrations is a monstrous ego that affirms its preeminence in acts of intellectual pride. He is referring to himself when he asks Op in Chapter 18, "Do you admit you've met your master, have run into a criminal too wily for you?" He needs the reassurance his question calls for. To compensate for his low readership, he founded the Grail cult and brought it to San Francisco; the novelist's imagination both pushes into and overtakes life after failing in the literary sphere. Imagination rules him so much that it has distorted his judgment. Even his fascination with Gabrielle is mental rather than sexual, riveting on the unusual appearance created by her low forehead, lobeless, fawn-like ears, and small, pointed teeth.

But he has more grit than he lets on, rivaling the Op in resolve and purpose. In order to stop Tom Fink from speaking out in front of Op in Chapter 18, he sets off the bomb Fink brought into the room. Just before this, he had strangled Daisy Cotton to death in Quesada. The same nerve and control help see him through his Iago-like resolve never to speak to Op after their last interview in the hospital. He also fights back from near-certain death after the explosion that put him in the hospital to begin with. He has instigated crimes; he has performed desperate crimes on his own. But his cunning runs to waste, his rebirth bringing only madness and mutilation. Fitzstephan survives as a burned-out, twisted wreck, half his body gone and his mind a small, dark place. It is fitting that someone who has turned life into a thought system should live on as a grotesque. It may also be too overtly moralistic. Fitzstephan stands up to Op throughout. Op's reference to him in Chapter 18 as "a mangled pile of flesh and clothing" and phrases like "the wreck of Fitzstephan" and "what was left of Fitzstephan" all suggest that Op knew of the novelist's guilt five chapters from the end. His heartless words carry the sting of condemnation. Yet Hammett interposes Gabrielle's morphine cure both to let Fitzstephan suffer horribly and to give Op the chance to charge him with his crimes while he lies bandage-swathed in a hospital bed.

The true meeting-ground of the detective and the criminal is twenty-year-old Gabrielle. Criminal and detective approach Gabrielle from different angles and with different goals. The detective pretends to have more interest in her than he does; the criminal pretends less. But whereas Fitzstephan's fascination makes him kill her doctor, her parents, and her husband, Op asks and takes nothing from her. Curiously, neither man wants her sexually. Perhaps Op and Fitzstephan know her better than the men who did lust after her—Joseph Haldorn and Eric Collinson. As Thompson's rehearsal of her troubled past shows, her mental problems make her an unpromising sexual partner:

> She has been psychically mutilated since childhood, having grown up hating her father and thinking him a murderer, losing her mother and gaining the twisted Alice as stepmother, turning to drugs for escape, having had her husband murdered, and believing that she killed her mother and feeling she lives under a curse for it. Twice since childhood she has attempted suicide.[2]

Nearly everyone in the book reacts magnetically to Gabrielle, wanting to control or exploit her; even the Leggetts' former housekeeper, who knew her as a small girl, calls her a "tartar" and refers to her always as "that Gabrielle." Along with her faintly aristocratic European background, these special claims make her a perfect Gothic heroine. Haldorn wants sex from her; lawyer Madison Andrews wants the fee connected with administering her estate; her stepmother tries to brand her with a family curse; following a pattern introduced in "The Assistant Murderer" (1926), Eric marries her at a time when she's too weak and confused to resist; both her stepmother and her spiritual adviser use her to commit murder; Eric's family wants to convict her for murdering Eric. She even mistreats herself; as has been seen, she tries suicide twice besides wrecking her constitution with morphine. Only Op treats her right, asking nothing in return. Yet his loving service both looks and feels like the work of hatred. No wonder she takes drugs; no wonder she's always disappearing. Not even safe from herself, she lives under constant nervous strain.

Although many readers have warmed to Gabrielle, very few give *Dain Curse* top marks. It is the only one of Hammett's novels, for instance, that Alvarez dislikes, calling it "wandering, melodramatic, a bit silly, and, with its supernatural trimmings, not at all typical."[3] Without discounting Alvarez's objection, we do question what he means by "typical." Perhaps the English critic prefers the urban depravity of a B-film about Capone's Chicago in the 1920s. Foreigners often wince when a real-life place doesn't fit the image of it put forth by books or films; witness the countless Americans who find to their chagrin that today's London lacks the cobbled streets, hansom cabs, and heavy, rolling fogs of Sherlock Holmes's heyday. If Alvarez wants his American detective fiction to resemble simplistic lower-depths journalism, then his contempt for *Dain Curse* makes sense. A more substantial disclaimer comes from the American critic Kenney: "It is Hammett's most elaborately plotted novel. Indeed, the elaboration . . . becomes excessive . . . . Continually, one has the impression that the characters are entirely at the service of the plot."[4]

Narrative flow, *Dain Curse* lacks; its driven people seem posed and arranged. But it isn't so wooden as it is segmented. It stops several times for letters or long explanations, whose information should have been conveyed in action. Also, the Queseda section (Part Three), with its sexual intrigue, political infighting, and remote setting, doesn't knit well with the rest. Hammett tries to smooth some of these snags by means of repetition. Revealingly, most of the repetition in *Dain Curse* refers to violence, ordering it and inviting meanings. The Op-Fitzstephan doubling resonates with the eternal love-hate opposition between the Dain sisters. Other repetitions include letters written by Edgar Leggett and Daisy Cotton just before they get murdered by Fitzstephan, the two scenes at either end of the book in which Aaronia

108

and Op ask each other to see Gabrielle, and murders at the ends of Parts One and Three. Finally, just as Alice Dain Leggett is shot in the throat, knife wounds in *his* throat kill Joseph Haldorn. Before these deaths, Alice had persuaded Gabrielle to shoot her mother, Lily. Then Fitzstephan uses Gabrielle's black maid, Minnie Hershey, to kill Dr. Riese. It's not accidental that the instigators of these two murders are the book's most evil characters. A cradle Catholic, Hammett must have known that the worst punishments in Dante's Hell fasten on people who destroy life for personal gain. The destroyer who uses others as instruments of destruction, by implicating them in his guilt, performs psychological homicide as well as murder. To befit his sin, his expiation (Dante's condign punishment) could reach agonizing intensities.

Hammett's insight flags, though, in his portrayal of weepy, superstitious, and generally ignorant Minnie Hershey. Referred to in the narrative sequences as the mulatto and in conversation by terms like shine, dinge, and the high yellow (terms also used in Chandler's *Farewell, My Lovely*), Minnie, who even has a last name suggesting chocolate, displays little of the earthy dignity accorded blacks by white writers of the day like Sherwood Anderson and Faulkner. In extenuation, though, one of Hammett's most cool, intelligent figures is Jack Bye, the black narrator of "Nightshade." But we needn't look to this 1933 story for offsetting virtues to the crude Minnie Hershey portrait. Thompson has shown how the appearance-reality dualism both creates and controls narrative tempo in *Dain Curse:*

> The Leggett jewel robbery turns out to be a phoney, Leggett's suicide turns out to be murder, his confession a tissue of manufactured lies, and Alice Dain Leggett's death, though it too appears to be an accident, is also murder. In Part Two, Gabrielle goes to the Temple of the Holy Grail for rest and psychic recovery . . . . But instead of recovery, she finds herself enmeshed in a twisted cult.[5]

Besides using this seem-be interplay to create unity, Hammett also provides a stunning crime puzzle. That the bomber of Chapter 18 suffers more from the bomb he ignites than anyone else makes him the least likely suspect, a stratagem that both prolongs the mystery and distributes suspicion among the other characters. Finally, the speed and accuracy of Hammett's prose strengthens the action. Particularly notable are the descriptions of brutalized women—the strangled corpse of Daisy Cotton in Queseda and the sneezing, twitching, and jerking movement of Gabrielle during the morphine cure. The descriptive brutality of these passages reveals Hammett invoking his dark side. It is as if he is relishing the brutality as he creates it, in the manner of lanky Fitzstephan, whom he resembles physically much more than the stubby Op.

Though style lends distinction to *Dain Curse,* it doesn't transform the work into a solid, serious novel. The choppy structure, uneven tone, and clumsy shifting of setting create problems beyond the reach of stylistic flair. Most of these problems come from the same source—the derailment of the action in Queseda, which either sidetracks the action for good or leaves the reader at the crowded terminal, behind and bewildered.

5

Sam Spade and Other Romantics

More than two generations of readers have made Hammett's Sam Spade their model of the hardboiled private eye. They have enshrined Spade without knowing much about him. What they have overlooked is his heart. His toughness is leavened by both tenderness and subtlety; he has a feminine sensitivity to atmospheres and textures. Though basically a man of action, he doesn't exhaust his personality in man-talk or high-speed movement. He even loves Brigid O'Shaughnessy because she satisfies his urbane needs; he and Brigid communicate more through gesture, nuance, and irony than through direct statement. The style of their relationship is hit straightaway when she comes into his office as Miss Wonderly. The success of her visit depends on her ability both to reveal and conceal information about her nonexistent sister, Corinne. From her garbled story—garbled by pretended psychological stress—Spade builds a plausible account of Corinne's troubles. The scene is a duel of wits. Playing out feeling while they suppress facts, both detective and client improvise brilliantly. Prophetic insight led Hammett to set *The Maltese Falcon* (1930) in what was to become America's most sophisticated city.

Hammett's complexity of insight brought new depths and tints to *Black Mask* fiction. These make *The Falcon* a subtle study of moral

111

behavior and of degrees of emotional commitment and stress. Though Edenbaum's definition of the private dick, or " 'daemonic' tough guy," comes straight from his reading of Hammett, it bypasses much that is important in Spade:

> He is free of sentiment, of the fear of death, of the temptations of money and sex . . . . He is capable of any action, without regard to conventional morality, and thus is apparently as amoral—or immoral—as his antagonists.[1]

Contra Edenbaum, sex and money both tempt Spade. And to call his possible corruption in the novel's last scene "patiently absurd,"[2] as Thompson does, is to miscue. Spade barely escapes contamination. He harbors guilty knowledge throughout, and only a combination of luck and resolve saves him at the end. When Captain Jacobi brought the lead facsimile of the Maltese falcon to his office, both men believed in the bird's authenticity, Jacobi confirming *his* belief by dying as he fulfills his mission. For such a prize, Spade, who holds no special brief with abstract truth or San Francisco law enforcement, would gladly pocket Gutman's $10,000. The $1,000 consolation prize he nips when Gutman tells him at gunpoint to return the fee he also wants.

Then why does he hand the bill over to the police at the end, along with Brigid, dismissing it nonchalantly as a bribe? Does the act confirm his moral purity? Or would keeping the money be foolish? Consider what this entails—risking his reputation, his license, perhaps even his freedom. He has angered both Lieutenant Bundy and District Attorney Bryan; either man would grab the chance to jail him. Consider, next, the odds favoring them. Although Gutman, the giver of the money, is dead, both Brigid and Joel Cairo have gone to jail; Wilmer Cook, still at large after killing Gutman, lacks both the cunning and the connections to elude the police for long. He, Cairo, and Brigid have all been arrested because of Spade. Moreover, all three saw Spade pocket Gutman's $1000 bill; all would testify with relish against Spade. And Spade knows it.

Thus, the $1000 is a luxury he can't afford. Despite his loose-living Marxist creator, he is very cautious and conservative. The parable of Flitcraft (Chapter 7) applies as vividly to him as to anybody else in the book. Flitcraft's feeble romantic protest against the chance ordering of things proves that character is fixed. Gutman and Cairo, captives both, remain spellbound by the falcon. Brigid keeps moving among

112

men and using sex to get what she wants from them. Flitcraft needs a family, a home in the suburbs, and a regular job; even his shattering revelation carries him only a short distance—from Tacoma to Spokane. The shock he gets from seeing life's injustice and horror wears off. Spade, too, is only moved briefly by the lure of easy money. Spade, too, reverts to his basic values and style. As several critics have said, he, unlike Flitcraft, lives in danger all the time; beams are always falling where he walks. In order to survive, he has to be alert. To relax, by trusting chance or another person, is to invite disaster. Had the street-wise, professional detective Spade craved Gutman's $1000, he'd still have steeled himself and renounced.

I

Restraint works for his self-preservation. Ross Macdonald includes Spade in his description of the novel's motivation:

> *The Maltese Falcon* is a fable of modern man in quest of love and money . . . . Its characters act out of the extreme emotions of fear and guilt and concupiscence, anger and revenge; and with such fidelity to these passions that their natures almost seem co-terminous with them.[3]

The questers for the falcon are so driven that they will circle the earth, bribe, betray, or kill for it. The bird's power to corrupt infects nearly everybody. Spade's secretary, Effie Perrine, says of her Uncle Ted, a professor at Berkeley whom she talked to about the bird, "He's all excited about it." Normally controlled and poised, Spade, too, sacrifices vision to the bird. So happy is he to be holding what he believes to be the real falcon that he squeezes Effie too hard and absentmindedly steps on the dead hand of Captain Jacobi, who had brought the figure to his office. But the figure also prompts sexual references, most of which occur near murder. Miles Archer dies in a dark, clammy alley during the night hours, the time of romance. Like Floyd Thursby, who gets four bullets in the back because of Brigid, Archer can't defend himself when lured into the moist, beckoning alley. Like Thursby, he dies when blinded by desire. To promote variety amid unity, Hammett has Archer wearing his pistol on his hip and puts Thursby's in his shoulder holster at the time of the shootings.

In each case, the undrawn pistol symbolizes helplessness. Both Thursby and Archer lust for Brigid. Beguiled to the point of inaction, both men die together with their demanning. Another of Brigid's sexual conquests and indirect murder victims, Captain Jacobi of the *Paloma,* drops dead in Chapter 16 while carrying a package with the phony lead falcon inside. (He, too, must have slept with Brigid to carry the falcon from Hong Kong to San Francisco.) Jacobi's holding himself "stiffly straight" while pitching to his death clinches the equation of sex and death. Whoever gets his head turned by Brigid, the book's Medusa-figure, risks being hardened into a corpse.

Brigid exerts force. She meets little resistance in Chapter 8 when she pistol-whips Joel Cairo; even a homosexual, whom she can't tempt with her favors, isn't able to keep her at bay. Naturally, the homosexual Cairo lacks integrity and substance for the *Black Mask* old boy, Hammett. But he isn't the only character who fails to live fully. The revolvers that are often drawn but rarely fired within our view also imply twisted, hammered-down male potency. Sexual failure or unreadiness prevades the book's nervous system. The youngest and most unformed character is the foulmouthed killer of Thursby and Jacobi, Wilmer Cook. Wilmer's high voice and scrawny wrists, his beardlessness and his youth, bar him, along with his cowardice (he shoots Thursby in the back), from manhood. Yet manhood is what he craves most; he will even kill to feel manly. The last murder he performs, though tossed in casually, tells most about Wilmer. For if the father is the key to the dissenter, or protester, then Wilmer's shooting of Casper Gutman, his bogus father, represents the son's ritual killing of the father preparatory to manhood. Spade's deadpan response to the news of the shooting murder captures the murder's ritual significance: "He [i.e., Gutman, who had exchanged Wilmer, his substitute son, for the falcon] ought to have expected that."

Spade reads Wilmer's heart because he, too, in his skirmishes with Lieutenant Dundy and District Attorney Bryan, kicks against the father—his punitive, obedience-exacting society. Next, Wilmer's first two murder victims, Thursby and Jacobi, both slept with Brigid. (Significantly, Wilmer doesn't shoot Miles Archer, who, never having made love to Brigid, needn't be supplanted.) If Spade's wresting away both of Wilmer's pistols didn't already earmark the detective as a murder victim, then his becoming Brigid's lover had surely roused Wilmer's blood-wrath. Spade knows that he blocks Wilmer's drive to manhood. Wilmer can hurt him. No sooner does he recognize his relationship with Wilmer to have drifted into the Oedipal orbit than he recommends throwing "the punk" to the police. Spade isn't safe with Wilmer prowling around.

Though we never enter the detective's mind, Spade's actions add up to a controlled, tested maturity. Brigid sleeps with him in Chapter 9, believing, wrongly, that she can win his loyalty and trust along with his body. As soon as he wakes up the next morning, he steals her apartment key. That keys are phallic symbols to Freud sharpens the meaning of Spade's act. Chapter Nine, which took place at night, was called "Brigid." Spade wakes up in the next chapter. His theft of the key in the first paragraph of Chapter 10 ends Bridgid's reign of darkness. Having seen daylight, he can renew the energy and self-being he had given up during the dark hours. He celebrates the renewal of his powers after successully searching Brigid's apartment by cooking a breakfast of eggs—symbolic of rebirth. Hammett identifies keys with consciousness and control, even power. Chapter Fourteen, which begins with Spade waking up after being drugged by Gutman, contains a passage as expressive of Spade's clarity and grip as the much-quoted cigarette-rolling ritual of Chapter 2. Could the passage in Chapter 14 also convey the hidden sexual fears of the tubercular, malnourished man who would write *The Glass Key* and then enlist in the Army for overseas duty at age forty-eight?[4]

> He put his hand on the knob and turned it with care that permitted neither rattle nor click. He turned the knob until it would would turn no further: the door was locked. Holding the knob still, he changed hands, taking it now in his left hand. With his right hand he brought his keys out of his pocket, carefully, so that they should not jingle against one another. He separated the office-key from the others and, smothering the others together in his palm, inserted the office-key in the lock. The insertion was soundless.

This key symbolism can be overrated as a descriptive tool. Spade doesn't turn every encounter he has with a woman into a sexual challenge; nor does he size up every woman he meets as a possible bedmate. Just as he carries no revolver, unless he is lying to Lieutenant Dundy in Chapter 2, so does his behavior with women belie Somerset Maugham's description of him as an "unscrupulous rogue and . . .

115

heartless crook."[5] He sneers at male authority-figures; he cracks wise with lawyers and other detectives. But he can extend both charity and charm to women without wanting something in return. He will rarely address Brigid or Effie Perrine, his secretary, without using terms of endearment, like "angel," "precious," or "darling." Afraid that Rhea Gutman, the fat man's daughter, may die from drugs if allowed to sleep, he walks and then runs her around her room. Then, before leaving her, he sets her gently on her bed, arranges her pillow and blankets, and phones for an ambulance. Does this compassion befit a rogue or a crook? Though anxious to find Brigid, he stays five more minutes with Rhea after she falls asleep to make sure she's breathing regularly.

He even acts the gentleman in his sexual relationships. Sex means more to him than erotic play; it also has an expressive function. Though Iva Archer's lover, he drops Iva as soon as Brigid comes along. He won't even break the news of her husband's death to Iva, and he neglects her so badly that she sends for her brother-in-law to make trouble for him. Should Spade be attacked for dropping Iva for somebody he likes better? Or should we commend him for knowing what he wants and then acting on his knowledge? In either case, he doesn't meet Iva's anger with anger. Instead, he acts with tact and thoughtfulness. He sends flowers for Miles's funeral. He changes the subject, assuring her that "it's all right now," when Iva explains how she tried to hurt him. He also forgives her (Chapter 11) both for lying about being home when Miles died and for sending the police to Brigid's apartment. Last, he kisses her and, calling her "poor darling," speaks softly to her ("His voice was tender") the first time they meet after Miles's death. His kindness reaps an ironic gain. The end of the book finds him back together with her; shivering, he tells Effie Perrine to send her into his office. He can accept her without liking her and can sympathize with her grief while feeling no grief himself. What is more, the ordeal of giving Brigid to the police has shaken him; he doesn't want to be alone. Since Effie has rejected him, he has to settle for Iva.

His being moved deeply enough to want company during his ordeal proves his humanity once again. Giving Brigid to the police isn't part of a normal day's work for him; Thompson refers correctly to "the depth of Spade's emotional strain."[6] Technique brings this strain to the fore. Now moral issues run to waste in fiction unless made individual and particular. Thus Hammett gets rid of Gutman, Cairo, and Wilmer at the end of Chapter 19 to leave Brigid alone with Spade. The last chapter sharpens to a one-to-one confrontation between the two main characters. Yet this final interview between the lovers doesn't narrow to a simplistic clash between a villainess who thrives on feeling and an unfeeling hero.[7] Such a clash wouldn't signify enough to provide a crescendo. And Chapter 20 is both crescendo *and* denouement. Spade has already struggled internally before justifying his arrest of Brigid; the "rotten nights" that will break his rest have already begun plaguing him. Though never reporting Spade's thoughts firsthand, Hammett does use gesture, facial expression, and dialogue to show Spade a battlefield of moral and romantic impulses. He is usually friendly with Effie Perrine, confiding in her and asking her advice. His tart rejoinder in Chapter 16 to her charge that he is mistreating Brigid suggests inner turmoil:

> "That's spite . . . . You're sore because she did something on her own hook, without telling you. Why shouldn't she? You're not so damned honest, and you haven't been so much on the level with her, that she should trust you completely."
> Spade said: "That's enough of that."

Spade suffers because he's betraying his principles. He knows enough to convict Brigid of murder early in the action. In Chapter 6, his clear, hard, steady look intimidates her: "He . . . looked at her with eyes that studied, weighed, judged her without pretense that they were not studying, weighing, judging her. She flushed slightly under the frankness of his scrutiny." Brigid stands in little danger of being arrested at this point. Spade's unreadiness to turn her in shows in his reciting the Flitcraft parable in the next chapter—perhaps to warn her indirectly that he may have to end their romance by jailing her? Verbal indirection and hard looks are all he can manage here. He hasn't overcome his feelings. Though his guilty knowledge is tormenting him, he can't arrest her. As has been seen, Flitcraft showed him the need to translate vision and conviction into action. His recounting of Flitcraft's story in Chapter 7 serves as a reminder, a prod, and an expression of self-disgust. He knows his duty. But he also knows that he is too weak to do it.

He is still foundering in the last chapter. The chapter begins, "For all of five minutes after the outer door had closed behind Casper Gutman and Joel Cairo, Spade, motionless, stood staring at the knob of the open living-room door.'' He hates his duty more than ever, since he can't postpone it any longer. The final interview puts him under awful stress. He frowns and grimaces; his usually inexpressive eyes burn wildly; his sweating face goes yellow and white with pain; he speaks in a strange new voice. Spade is no angry avenger. He can't shut out love; even while explaining systematically why he must turn Brigid in, he eyes her "hungrily." He is telling the truth when he claims to have known from the start that she killed Miles Archer. His freeing his partner's killer violates the ritual code of his trade: "When one of your organization gets killed it's bad business to let the killer get away with it. It's bad all around—bad for that one organization, bad for every detective everywhere," he tells Brigid at the end. Like the Flitcraft story, his tidy catalog of seven reasons why Brigid belongs in jail shames him into arresting her. He has resisted "turning her over" for eighteen chapters because he loves her. Instead of calling the police, he has made excuses for her, overlooked her lies, and continually tried to help her help *him*. He sides with her throughout. Chapter Four shows him groping for a way to protect her: "I've got nothing against trusting you blindly except that I won't be able to do you much good if I haven't some idea of what it's all about." Chapter Six finds his moral commitment to her unshaken. Although she has given him two false names, invented a story about a fictional sister, suppressed information about the Maltese falcon, *and* killed his partner, he still wants to trust and help her: "I'm willing to help you. I've done what I could so far. If necessary I'll go ahead blindfolded, but I can't do it without more confidence in you than I've got now." Even in Chapter 7, he tells her, "You don't have to trust me . . . as long as you can persuade me to trust you." Clearly, he is stalling for time. He is giving her every chance to tell him something he can live with, to the point of telling a lie that won't insult his intelligence. His angry charge, that she doesn't know what it's all about, refers to her failure to answer his veiled appeal for comfort.

Spade's love for Brigid touches our hearts. She has positively enchanted the detective. Her throwing herself at his mercy in Chapter 4—which she does because Spade won't say that he believes her innocent of the Thursby and Archer murders—moves him as deeply as it must have Thursby and Captain Jacobi. He is left literally breathless:

118

> She went down on her knees at his knees . . . "Oh, I'm so alone and afraid, and I've got nobody to help me if you won't help me. I know I've no right to ask you to trust me if I won't trust you. I do trust you, but I can't tell you. I can't tell you now . . . . Mr. Spade, don't ask me to be fair. You're strong, you're resourceful, you're brave. You can spare me some of that strength and resourcefulness and courage, surely. Help me, Mr. Spade. Help me because I need help so badly . . . ."
>
> Spade, who had held his breath through much of this speech, now emptied his lungs with a long sighing exhalation between pursed lips and said: "You won't need much of anybody's help. You're good. You're very good."

His repeating in Chapter 6, "You're good. You're very good," conveys the same breathless admiration. For self-protection, he has to twist and hammer her magic down to a virtuoso performance while planning his next move. Not only does Spade love Brigid; he also believes that they are well suited. He is probably right. Both of them enjoy communicating through nuance; both like to skirt the fringes of the law; above all, each touches a central nerve in the other. The subtle verbal byplay they generate amid wavelets of sexual arousal prefigures the loving, sparkling repartee of Nick and Nora Charles in *The Thin Man*. In their short time together, Brigid has delighted, vexed, and won him, making good the transforming power hinted at by her front name. Losing her points the loss of many key hopes and opportunities.

These hopes and opportunities matter. Since Spade stands as Hammett's ace prototype of the private eye, his loss conveys the frustration and self-denial intrinsic to his job. "He is what most of the private detectives I worked with would like to have been," said Hammett of him in 1934. "Your private detective does not . . . want to be an erudite solver of riddles in the Sherlock Holmes manner; he wants to be a hard and shifty fellow, able to take care of himself in any situation, able to get the best of anybody he comes in contact with, whether criminal, innocent by-stander, or client."[8] Thus Joel Cairo tells Spade in Chapter 10, "You always have, I must say, a smooth explanation ready." Smooth explanations call for poise and self-command, two outstanding traits in a man whose livelihood rests on concealments, evasions, and bluffs. From the start, Spade faces heavy pressure; the police think him guilty of killing Floyd Thursby, and Iva Archer

119

believes him to be Miles's killer. Yet he relieves the pressure created by these suspicions, his training and skill helping him reconstruct Miles's murder in Chapter 2 just as he had reconstructed Brigid's imaginary plight in Chapter 1. Rarely, will he give anything away in an interview that he wants to hold back. At tense moments, he will either rid his voice and face of expression or throw his interlocutor off balance with a facial contortion. Hammett says of him, during his first interview with Brigid after the Archer murder, "The upper part of his face frowned. The lower part smiled." This ambivalence confuses her, and thus, gives him the upper hand. Much of the street sense that prompted it comes from experience, which, in his case, means prior mistakes. For instance, he knows the value of restraint from not having restrained himself with Iva, who expects him to marry her now that Miles is dead. Predictably, in Sid Wise (whose name was carefully chosen) Spade has a lawyer who can be trusted to bury secrets and avoid embarrassing truths; there are no indiscreet questions, only indiscreet answers. On the other hand, Miles Archer has forfeited Spade's trust because he talks too much, making direct statements of fact in his "heavy, coarse" voice. His lack of reserve gives him an upfront quality that precludes confidence. As soon as he sees Brigid, he begins ogling her. His leaping at the chance to meet her that evening brings home the error of his impulsiveness; for, had he not acted so hastily, he'd not have been decoyed into a dark alley and shot. When told by Spade, "You've got brains," he's too thick-witted, rocking smugly on his heels, to see the irony.

Irony helps Spade survive, along with his common sense and instinct for timing. As shrewd and crafty as he is, though, Brigid keeps pace with him most of the way. Not only is she a fine actress; like Spade, she also knows how to time her best effects. She only goes into her melodramatic recital in Chapter 4 after failing to get him to say that he believes her innocent of the Archer and Thursby murders. Another brilliant improvisation follows in Chapter 8. When some shrieks of pain from Joel Cairo bring the policemen, Dundy and Polhaus, into Spade's apartment, she assumes a foetal posture in order to look innocent and helpless. The improvisation works. Though Cairo's lip and forehead are both bleeding, she persuades the police that she, not he, was the victim in their scuffle. She even gets away with slapping and kicking him in the police's presence. Had the innocent Cairo struck out at her like this, he'd have been stopped before landing a blow.

Spade can't be fooled as easily as the police. Her calling this controlled, poised man wild and unpredictable shows him that either she doesn't know him or she is trying to lower his guard with flattery. Neither response chimes with the love she set up as a moral touchstone for their behavior with each other. Call her hypocrite. Love meant nothing to her, first, when the arrival of the *Paloma,* with the falcon on board, turned her from him and, next, when she delivered him unarmed to the Gutman gang, after a search of the *Paloma* failed to uncover the statuette. Spade did well to turn her over to the police; for one thing, only in prison would she be unable to tempt him. Although we share his loss, we also approve of his action. But our approval is both grudging and detached: life shimmers and pulses less without Brigid. A tragedy of lost hopes and chances, *The Maltese Falcon* shows life sustaining itself both at a reduced level and at a great cost. With Brigid, Spade not only glimpsed Paradise; he also enjoyed it. As such, he knows all too well the value of that which his sense of self-preservation has rejected.

No wonder his last talk with her finds him so sweating and so badgered. As is reflected in his violence with Wilmer Cook, his bottled-up frustration seeks outlets. He is cruel because he is in pain; though his duty is clear, he rejects it emotionally. A calculating machine or a rogue wouldn't feel this stress; nor would one have fascinated two generations of readers. Like Chandler's Philip Marlowe and Ross Macdonald's Lew Archer after him, Spade will bend the law, risk his license, or take a beating in the line of work. No slave to facts and proofs, he will also softpedal the truth for a client or a friend: Brigid's $200 retainer in Chapter 1 erases any moral blame attaching to her lies; in Chapter 4 he tells her, "We ought to be able to fake a story that will rock them [the police] to sleep, if necessary." His practice of not carrying a gun reveals an openness and generosity of spirit that overrides hardboiled literary detection. His conduct with Brigid and the police, with whom he always shakes hands, reflects his good-natured awareness that every business transaction is also a social encounter. Spade knows how to relax and enjoy. Life contains more for him than hustlers and suckers; he feels no need to beat the bushes for enemies.

But enemies he has, and his survival depends on reducing their power over him. Like much of American fiction, *Falcon* leans heavily

121

on the head-heart dualism. But Hammett oposes the Hawthorne of "Young Goodman Brown" and *The Scarlet Letter* and the Faulkner of *Light in August* by rating reason over emotion. Spade's reason tells him to go against his heart, and, by acting reasonably, he survives. *Falcon* fits William Ruehlmann's description of the private eye novel as "a Western that took place somewhere else."[9] Both the work's time-setting and geographical setting slant Spade's morality toward that of frontier fiction. San Francisco, or at least Spade's San Francisco, is more of a pioneer outpost than a civilized city: a civilization balances male and female principles, and no such balance obtains in the novel. San Francisco exudes violence; as Ross Macdonald said, money-lust and concupiscence rule the characters.[10] "So much for your intuition," Spade tells Effie on the last page; her faith in Brigid has been wrongheaded. Analogously, many of the other female virtues either misfire or miscarry in this hard, fighting town. The comfort and healing warmth that Iva should be bestowing upon Miles, her husband, she lavishes upon Spade, her lover. Brigid stands for sexual love, trust, and mercy. Yet she perverts these values; her breathtaking performance as a helpless sinner merely masks her greed. Joel Cairo's homosexuality reflects the sickness of the metropolis, not its energy. The imaginative commitment to unrevealed life normally connected with the female principle goes for nil. Nobody wants the falcon for its beauty; religion spurs no one; friendship carries a price tag.

II

Its eccentric form stops *Falcon* from being a whodunit. *Falcon* is a psychological novel with almost no psychology. Only at the end do its structure and motivation reveal themselves. Brigid's overthrow still frets Spade through most of the last sequence. His indecisiveness has fretted him since Chapter 2, where he found Miles's corpse. But what happens at the end to rouse him to action? Help comes from an unexpected source. The discovery that a thousand-dollar bill has been pinched from Gutman's envelope in Chapter 19 gives Spade's flagging instinct for self-preservation a needed boost. The detective seizes his chance quickly, forcing Brigid to undress in the bathroom, allegedly to make sure she didn't hide the money on her person. She accuses him of killing something—the dark, wordless love bond joining them. Ironically, this is Spade's purpose. His saying, "Now I know," after inspecting her clothes, refers to his faith in his ability to arrest Brigid. He has known all along that she didn't take the money. He also knows that bringing his sexual bond with Brigid into the harsh porcelain glare of his bathroom (the same room in which he stole her apartment key in Chapter 10), with Gutman and Cairo sitting within earshot, will weaken the bond. Seeing her naked and feeling no sexual arousal marks the first victory of his reason over his heart. Not once in the exchange does he touch her. Having reduced her to a visual object, he can now throw her to the police.

In police custody is where she belongs. She killed Miles Archer. She betrayed both Gutman and Kemidov, the Russian general she had met in Constantinople, with Cairo. Then, after betraying Cairo with Thursby, she betrayed Thursby with Captain Jacobi. (Also included in her scheme to get rich was the Constantinople boy Cairo says she couldn't make in Chapter 7.) Of these men, only Kemidov and Cairo are still alive, Cairo barely; in Chapter 8, after pistol-whipping him, Brigid was about to shoot him when stopped by Spade and the police. Miles Archer she did shoot. Not only do men she knows sometimes turn up dead; Archer and Thursby also prove that loving or even trusting Brigid can be fatal:

> "That's a lie," Spade said. "You had Thursby hooked and you knew it. He was a sucker for women. His record shows that—the only falls he took were over women."

*　　　　　*　　　　　*

> Spade smiled wolfishly . . . . "Miles hadn't many brains, but, Christ! he had too many years' experience as a detective to be caught . . . by the man he was shadowing. Up a blind alley with his gun tucked away on his hip and his overcoat buttoned? Not a chance . . . . You'd told us Thursby was a bad actor. He couldn't have tricked Miles into the alley like that, and he couldn't have driven him in."

This treachery ends the lovers' shadow game of psychological suggestion. As has been seen, the novel's riveting moral issue has not been Brigid's guilt but, rather, Spade's inability to act on it. Brigid's treachery strengthens his resolve. Although he can cope with dishonesty and even murder, he won't tolerate sexual betrayal. Experience has proved her unworthy of his romantic idealism:

123

Spade made a short abrupt bow . . . "I should trust you . . .? You who knocked off Miles, a man you had nothing against, in cold blood . . . ? You who double-crossed Gutman, Cairo, Thursby—one, two, three? You who've never played square with me for half an hour at a stretch since I've known you?"

Fear of playing the sap or the sucker clinches his argument. To mix reason and sentiment is to deny reason. Like Flitcraft, his "spiritual twin,"[11] he parts company but briefly with the realities governing his life. The speed with which this conservative man sides with Brigid provokes a reaction which shows him to be harsher with himself than with others. Part of his anger in his last interview with her is self-directed for surrendering grip as long as he did.

The book's last paragraph finds him standing beside his office desk. He has regained his coping power and, along with it, a firm hold on his basic values. These are always near at hand, easily identifiable, and bound up with a system or code. He lives in the present amid tangible facts. The detective's code and training helps him make sense of these facts. Alive to surfaces, weights, and measures—the thinginess of things—he knows how to handle physical substances. His ability to search an apartment, roll a cigarette, or slide a key into a lock noiselessly makes him a master of perceptible reality. Any amateur who tries to search him at gunpoint, as Cairo does in Chapter 5, will soon be sprawling on the floor and looking up the bore of his own revolver.

Accompanying the restoration of his expertise and the bleak discipline serving it is Iva Archer. An ironic look over his shoulder at his lost hopes makes Spade shiver as he prepares to greet Iva; Iva has brought a chill into the office. No good detective can afford either the outgoings or the risks of sexual love. Spade can't undo his conduct with Brigid, who could have renewed him. But, treacherous and self-serving, she also could have killed him. He won't love again. Iva, who appeals to him on a shallow, physical level, fits his refurbished self-image. She is the perfect match for a romantic cynic. She will never jar Spade's style or attitudes. Nor can she stir his heart. Can he be blamed for shuddering with wry regret as he renounces love to harden into the prototype of the unfeeling private eye?

124

III

The feeling and the meaning of Hammett's most popular and enduring work inheres not in what the people do but why they do it. The main thrust of the Flitcraft story, for instance, comes in Spade's reason for telling it—to advise Brigid indirectly that, bedazzled though he may be for the moment, he will revert to the mentality of the private detective and arrest her for murdering Miles Archer, unless she talks him out of it. The chance he offers her is small, but real, and she should have grabbed it. She should have also caught his drift; the two of them twist, lie, and conceal frequently. For example, Spade always feigns amiability and compassion when he sees Iva. Also, by rifling Brigid's apartment in Chapter 10, he gives the impression that Brigid is in danger. Then he uses the danger he has manufactured to persuade Effie to put her up for a few days. He stows Brigid with Effie because, distrusting her, he doesn't want her talking to anybody about the bird. Brigid, though, answers his deception with one of her own—secretly meeting the *Paloma,* which just docked in San Francisco harbor, in order to pry the falcon from its captain. The maneuver is calculated. Rarely are Hammett's self-serving liars taken in by their lies and treacheries. Rather, practiced hands at dissembling, they know the limits of their fabrications. Gutman, for instance, uses talk in the same way that Brigid uses sex—to lower Spade's guard. At the same time, this brilliant speaker understands the limits of speech. When Spade compares the $10,000 Gutman offers him to the fat man's original offer, he is answered, "We were talking then. This is actual money, genuine coin of the realm, sir. With a dollar of this you can buy more than with ten dollars of talk." Brigid, too, acknowledges the limits of *her* powers by attacking Cairo when he refers, in Spade's presence, to somebody she allegedly couldn't make; she can't have her sexual charms impugned in front of the man she wants to use them on.

But Brigid and the others often map out their lying strategies away from us. The partnership between reader and writer is less confidential in *Falcon* than in most works of fiction. Abandoning the impressionism of the Op stories in favor of techniques that foreshadow the post-existentialist French novel, Hammett avoids connections and explanations, especially those pertaining to motives. Furthermore, his chapter titles will sometimes refer to side issues rather than major developments, and he will only report (in Chapters 2 and 11) one side of telephone conversations. The first two paragraphs of Chapter 2 display this objective realism at its most audacious:

> A telephone-bell rang in darkness. When it had rung three times bed-springs creaked, fingers fumbled on wood, something small and hard thudded on a carpeted floor, the springs creaked again, and a man's voice said:
> "Hello . . . Yes, speaking . . . Dead? . . . Yes . . . Fifteen minutes. Thanks."

Perhaps the last word of the chapter's title, "Death in the Fog," describes the mists through which the action reaches the reader. Not only is Archer murdered in a dark, fog-shrouded alley; his murder also reaches us indirectly. The events described in the first paragraph of the chapter relate to no perceiver other than the reader, and even *he* is kept literally in the dark; not until the fifth paragraph does he learn that the "man's voice" belongs to Spade. Also, by reporting only Spade's side of the phone conversation, Hammett can delay saying that the death that took the detective from his bed at two o'clock in the morning was that of his partner. We must read on to discover the identity of the murderee.

An event at the end of the next chapter shows again how Hammett's manipulation of the reader-writer partnership serves immediacy. The event reveals its force and meaning when compared to a similar one in the Op story, "The Whosis Kid" (1926). While the Op is shadowing the Kid, a messenger from the Continental brings him a memorandum containing information about his quarry. Op reads the memo, returns it, and explains his action to us: "After I had read the memorandum, I gave it back to the boy—there's no wisdom in carrying around a pocketful of stuff relating to your job." Chapter Three of *Falcon* ends with roughly the same kind of exchange. But here Hammett's detective, superbly mindless of his role as a literary character, bypasses explanations:

> The girl picked up a slip of paper from her desk and read the memorandum penciled on it. . . .
> Spade said, "Give me," and held out his hand. When she had given him the memorandum he took out his lighter, snapped on the flame, held the paper until all but one corner was curling black ash, dropped it on the linoleum floor, and mashed it under his shoe sole.

126

The girl watched him with disapproving eyes.

He grinned at her, said, "That's just the way it is, dear," and went out again.

The gap that the reader must fill in Chapter 5, which describes part of Spade's first meeting with Joel Cairo, is more emotional than intellectual. Spade has just taken Cairo's pistol away from him after Cairo's bungled attempt to hold the detective up. To teach Cairo a lesson, Spade smashes his face. But the smashing isn't shaped to the conventions of prose narrative. Drained or cleansed of any subjective response, the knockout punch comes to us as a deadpan recitation of surface details. Knocking out a holdup man is part of a day's work to the trained gumshoe, Spade. The sensation running up his arm as he punches Cairo tells less about him than the speed, timing, and accuracy of his knockout wallop. Even his rare moments of violence reflect the systematic thoroughness with which he works.

Whenever possible, Hammett will display this slow, methodical precision. Whatever glamor his displays forfeit, they make up for in honesty and naturalness, Spade's survival depending more on thoroughness than on heroics. Hammett makes the point stylistically in his description of Spade's search of Brigid's apartment in Chapter 10. Just as the passive verbs in the first two sentences stifle any personal response to the details at hand, so does the parallel structure in the next sentences, with pronoun subject and main verb coming at the onset, block dramatic heightening. The technique of giving Spade's various actions equal rhetorical value conveys his professional absorption in all the details of his job:

> Every drawer, cupboard, cubbyhole, box, bag, trunk—locked or unlocked—was opened and its contents subjected to examination by eyes and fingers. Every piece of clothing was tested by hands that felt for tell-tale bulges. . . . He stripped the bed of bedclothes. He looked under rugs. . . .He pulled down blinds. . . . He leaned through windows. . . . He poked. . . . He held. . . . He examined . . . .He emptied . . . . He opened . . . .

Very few literary works manipulate the reader as much as *Falcon*. A manual of detection, the novel also sustains tension while avoiding the on-stage portrayal of violence; Archer, Thursby, and Gutman are all killed out of view. Most boldly, it maneuvers us into identifying with

127

Brigid, the murderess. Like her, we can't believe that Spade will turn her over, even while he explains why he must. *Falcon* has many of the riggings of a conventional mystery—murder, sex, foreign intrigue—and a tough detective. But it puts these riggings to new uses. An understanding of Spade's motives—to survive and to make money—shows that the book avoids neither climaxes nor key issues. What looks like indirection is often a refocussing of emphasis; the realities of Spade's job feature responses treated periphally in other detective novels. *Falcon* is not usually read with an eye to Hammett's realignment of narrative priorities, the book's interests running counter to the spirit and purpose of most adventure writing. Also, Spade's desolation at the end tallies the cost of his professionalism, the novel's main subject; anyone who must keep watching for falling beams can't live at full stretch. Like Lawrence's *Women in Love* and Virginia Woolf's *To the Lighthouse,* both of which came out the same decade as *Falcon,* Hammett's best book criticizes a vision while imparting and celebrating it. Though Moss is correct when he argues that the book lacks a fast pace, he misfires badly by calling it "probably his [i.e., Hammett's] worst"[12] novel. The action the novel describes matters less than the reactions—professional and moral—it provokes; Spade, whose job denies him the luxury of moral behavior, and his counterparts all reveal themselves most vividly in their responses to the drama bred by the elusive falcon. These revelations display rare control, substance, and consistency. On the basis of them, *The Maltese Falcon* deserves to be called, as Kenney calls it, "one of the remarkable achievements of American crime fiction."[13]

128

6

City Lights

In the words of J.B. Priestley, *The Glass Key* is "a genuine novel of violence and city politics in the gangster era."[1] As usual in Hammett, the police, the District Attorney, and the press have all been bought off by local robber barons. Sex is again a force, as well; "Women, Politics, and Murder," the original title of the 1924 Hammett story, "Death on Pine Street," fits his 1931 novel as neatly as it does any number of his other works. But *Glass Key* also differs significantly from its counterparts. The novel describes the clash between rival gangs, both of which want to run the nameless eastern city, identified by Joe Gores as Baltimore,[2] where most of the action takes place. The buying off of the judges, police, and media has ruled out any moral or ideological clash between lawmen and outlaws; each of the rival gangs wants to control municipal graft, not end it. Like *Red Harvest* and *Falcon* before it, *Glass Key* describes battles of wit and courage rather than of right and wrong. Ethics aren't at stake. The book's main character, Ned Beaumont, works for a city boss whose morality and aims equal those of his rival. Lacking a social conscience, Beaumont and his chief don't care about relieving pain and stress; feeding the hungry, healing the sick, and finding work for the jobless mean nothing to them. Thirst for power, fast money, and manipulation drew them into politics, not humanitarian principles.

129

But power and its dynamics have changed since *Red Harvest,* acquiring a gloss of gentility in the move from the mountain west to the eastern seaboard. Political thugs act, talk, and dress more like gentlemen than like cowboys or gutter rats. Ned Beaumont lives amid trappings of quiet elegance; his chief's well-groomed rival wears dapper, conservative clothes and speaks in a soft musical brogue. These signs of good breeding are affected to impress local women's clubs, which control votes and public opinion. Beaumont's chief, tweed-garbed Paul Madvig, has geared his candidates' campaign to the city's vested interests, men and women who clawed their way to the top long enough ago to qualify as landed gentry, even though their prominence rests on guilt and betrayal. Hammett's eastern aristocracy lacks the principles to go along with its privilege. A city boss who aims at social prestige can be used and then dropped by the veteran politician he helped get elected. This politician, the book's most prominent, dignified-looking figure, is also the most corrupt, using his daughter as a sexual pawn and killing his son in order to get re-elected. In *Glass Key,* the Marxist novelist, Hammett, accepts corruption and vice as facts of urban life. Greed has overtaken all, the good manners and fine tailored clothes of the rich barely masking their lust for power and control.

I

Conveying both the diversity and complexity of the modern American city, *Glass Key* is a novel of interweaving ties. Politics knit with the family; business, friendship, and sex compete for the characters' loyalty; as has been seen, the power game rubs the class game. *Glass Key* offers both a more complex and more modern metaphor of urban life than *Red Harvest,* Hammett's other novel of municipal graft. City boss, Paul Madvig, whose mother speaks fluent but ungrammatical English, is backing the aristocratic Senator Ralph Henry for re-election. He also wants to marry the Senator's daughter, Janet, whom he fell in love with at first sight. Blocking Madvig's road to his twin goals is the romance of his daughter, Opal, with the Senator's son, Taylor. Madvig wants the romance stopped, believing Opal too young to take care of herself in an entanglement with a member of the gentry (a caution that, ironically, applies more strictly to him than to her). Though his wish is granted, it causes more

130

problems than it solves; Taylor Henry is found dead by Beaumont on a dark, wet, lonely street two blocks from Madvig's gambling casino. Madvig learns of other, related problems facing him from Beaumont, his best friend and chief adviser for the past year. Beaumont tells him that, since he wasn't invited to her birthday party, Madvig shouldn't buy Janet a gift; but if he can't resist, he mustn't get anything more commital than flowers. What is more, Beaumont continues, Madvig should withdraw his support from her father, who could never get elected without it.

The verbal exchange between the two men is typical. Though kindly and generous, Madvig sometimes lacks imagination; that a person with his Slav-sounding last name can marry Senator Ralph Bancroft Henry's daughter says more about the new social mobility of the times than about his understanding of Janet. Madvig does have the wit, though, to value Beaumont both as a conscience and a vessel of good sense. "I've never lost anything listening to you," he tells Beaumont, who advises him on a range of subjects including clothes, daughter-raising, business, and politics. Sometimes, Beaumont raises questions with Madvig before the police do in order to forestall trouble. Though blond, bulky Madvig finds some of these questions offensive, he usually deals with them as advised and thus draws their sting. On the other hand, rejecting Beaumont's advice will bring on trouble. The two men team well, taking turns helping each other in the early chapters. That some of the help is rejected doesn't erase its merit. Beaumont's advice about dropping the Senator shows real wisdom, as Madvig, who foolishly scorns it, will learn. Then Madvig loans Beaumont money to gamble with and appoints him the D.A.'s special investigator. These two favors are related, gambling troubles having made Beaumont ask for the appointment to begin with.

The bookmaker from whom he won $3250 on a horse race, to end a long slump, has left town. Beaumont follows him, carrying credentials from the D.A.'s office. These credentials can't be impugned. While they give him leverage with Bernie Despain, the welshing bookie, they also have a basis in law. Despain bolted with $1200 in unpaid IOU's from Taylor Henry in his safe. Thus Despain had a motive for murder. The second chapter, called "The Hat Trick," shows Beaumont going to New York with a "hat that did not quite fit him." The hat, which Opal, Taylor's former lover, got for him, helps him force Despain to pay his debt. Beaumont's success in getting his money

131

displays one of his most valuable assets, a stubborn integrity. Undaunted by a pounding given him by Despain's bodyguard, he goes to the bookie's hotel room the next day and stuffs Taylor's hat behind the cushion of a chair. The strategy works. Already suspected of killing Taylor, Despain prefers paying Beaumont his money to having the police find the hat where it was planted. We share Despain's shock when he discovers that he has been framed. The shock, one of the book's best effects, stems from shrewd narrative strategy. Though Beaumont noticed no hat near Taylor's corpse, he said nothing about it; the only link between his seeing no hat belonging to Taylor on this rainy night, his request that Opal get him one of Taylor's hats, and the framing of Despain is the repetition of the phrase, "the [or a] hat that did not quite fit him." As usual Hammett doesn't waste a detail, his curious, oft-repeated phrase furnishing an important help in our charting of Beaumont's hat strategy. What he loses in irony, he gains in impact. Despain's helplessness reaches us first hand, along with the discovery that Beaumont, who has punished the bookie for his villainy, exerts real force.

He will need all the force he can muster. "I wish to Christ the election was either over or further away," Madvig tells him upon his return home. While Beaumont was in New York, Madvig's rivals began a campaign to smirch his slate of candidates. Also, messages consisting of three questions typed identically on the same machine and linking Madvig to Taylor Henry's death are turning up in key places. Here is the one addressed to the D.A.:

> Why did Paul Madvig steal one of Taylor Henry's hats after he was murdered?
> What became of the hat that Taylor Henry was wearing when he was murdered?
> Why was the man who claimed to have first found Taylor Henry's body made a member of your staff?

Still more trouble enters the novel near the end of Chapter III with a new character named Shad O'Rory, a local speakeasy operator and political foe of Madvig. In his rich baritone, O'Rory complains that the upcoming election has made Madvig forget the differences between business and politics. Policemen O'Rory has bought off are closing his speakeasies rather than giving him the protection he paid for. Madvig won't call them off. In fact, he phones the local police chief and tells him, in O'Rory's presence, to prepare a raid on a speakeasy O'Rory talked about reopening.

The two ganglords aren't the only ones affected by their quarrel. After telling Madvig that he caused blood to flow by cornering O'Rory and then blocking his line of retreat, Beaumont announces his intentions to leave town. He doesn't want to stay for the bloodshed. In a scene that may have been staged for the benefit of O'Rory's partisans, he quarrels hotly with Madvig and punches him in the mouth when Madvig tries to stop him from walking away. Regardless of whether the defection is real or imagined, O'Rory hears of it and asks to see Beaumont. His motive? To get incriminating information to use against Madvig's candidates, the incumbents, in the election. With a breeze, Beaumont agrees to betray his ex-chief, but on his own terms. O'Rory has terms, too. Wanting to keep Beaumont's defection a secret, he insists that he and Beaumont map out their battle plan at his place. Beaumont is just as adamant. After serving notice that business will be done his way or not at all, he starts to leave. His refusal to bend—on a small issue, at that—costs him dearly; after O'Rory's bulldog drags him to the floor, the apelike henchman, Jeff Gardner, batters him mercilessly—both to discourage any further attempt to leave and to make him talk. This cruelty is ineffective. Jeff's slapping, kicking, punching, and bouncing of Beaumont fails to unearth information. Displaying either a monumental stubbornness or loyalty to Madvig, Beaumont remains silent. He also escapes his captors by dropping blindly from the window of a room where he is stowed after burning his original cell.

He wakes up to learn that he has been lying unconscious in a local hospital for three days. His first waking act consists of asking to see Madvig. Why? Was his fight with Madvig a hoax? Or did his stint with Shad O'Rory change his mind about breaking with his former chief? Because Hammett skirts the whole matter of motivation, he leaves these questions unanswered. Perhaps making himself up as he goes along, like a hero in an existential novel, Beaumont rejoins Madvig, saying tersely about the madness at O'Rory's, "I went there to lay a trap for the gent and he out-trapped me." In any case, Madvig doesn't question Beaumont's loyalty. The next day, he brings Janet Henry, the Senator's daughter, to the hospital. Janet's visit, a key scene, shows Hammett conveying idea through narrative structure. According to a count of its numbered units, or subchapters, the ten-chapter

Glass Key reaches its midpoint at the end of Chapter V, subchapter 2, and not at the end of the last subchapter of Chapter V. Beaumont has been unconscious for three days. Coinciding with his return to waking life, or rebirth, after Jeff Gardner's pounding, is the appearance of Janet, whom he meets in Chapter V, subchapter 3, i.e., at the outset of the novel's second half. The chatter he had lavished on her when he heard that she and Madvig were waiting to see him betrays a strong interest. After this chatter, the nonchalance he affects for her entrance can't hide his excitement from us. Or from her? Determined to make an impression, he and she begin baiting each other romantically as soon as they meet. Their erotic teasing continues till his irony sends her out of the room in tears. Her kittenish insistence that he doesn't like her had provoked him to retort with an insincerity of his own: "I'm kind of awkward and clumsy," he says, "when I'm around people like you who belong to another world altogether—society and roto-sections and all—and you mistake that—uh—*gaucherie* for enmity, which it isn't at all." Gauche is exactly what he is not, and both he and Janet know it. Their tantalizing exchange has been productive. Without a word of commitment, each has shown the other that he/she cares. Beaumont's nurse knows straightaway that they have clicked. When a basket of fruit arrives in his room the next day, she says, "I bet you it's from her." She is right. Beaumont, who later turns another woman's head in front of the woman's husband, knows how to use his charms.

He will soon have to display all his skills, including that of charm, as the novel's tempo quickens. Chapter Seven introduces Janet's father, the patrician Senator, with whom Beaumont will have to deal at several levels. Knowing that he needs Madvig to get re-elected, Senator Henry has told Janet to encourage him (for which action Beaumont later calls him a pimp). Janet, who believes that Madvig killed her brother and therefore hates him, strikes out the only way she can—indirectly. In order to vex him, she has been writing the anonymous letters consisting of three typed questions.

Madvig denies that both Janet and her father plan to drop him after election day. He may not have to wait this long, for his hopes are dimming elsewhere. His opponents have stirred up the public about the Taylor Henry murder. Unless the police, who are controlled by Madvig, solve the murder quickly, the Senator will lose at the polls. Some of his backers have already withdrawn their support. Picture Madvig's plight. He doesn't want to endanger his candidate, who is also, he hopes, his future father-in-law. But he doesn't want to lose Janet, either. In a surprising turn, he says that he accidentally killed Taylor during their quarrel, but that he has told nobody about it because he didn't want to destroy his chances with Janet. Beaumont reproaches him, but on the grounds of expediency, not morality, in keeping with the book's bitter spirit. Not only did Madvig sacrifice a self-defense plea by remaining silent; he also risked his safety for nothing. Janet Henry, the woman he loves and wants to marry, has always blamed him for her brother's death and has now convinced Opal of his guilt. As has been said, Madvig values Beaumont as his confidante-adviser because Beaumont, not afraid of delivering bad news, has always told him things that nobody else would. But Madvig can't bear hearing from anybody that Janet hates him enough to turn Opal against him. He fires Beaumont on the spot.

The detective element, i.e., the investigation of Taylor's murder, begins here in Chapter VIII and motorizes the novel the rest of the way. Detection comes late to *Glass Key,* a work often mistakenly called a mystery, because Beaumont had to break with Madvig before exploring his guilt or taking away his woman. Janet helps him all she can with the latter task. In fact, she has been helping him since their first meeting. Some of this encouragement wants touching in. Her tearful exit from his hospital room in Chapter V was only the start of her campaign to win his heart. This campaign took shape quickly. Wasting no time, she sent him some books after receiving a thank-you note for the flowers; interestingly, Beaumont, a master of protocol, had advised Madvig to make flowers *his* first gift to Janet when Madvig first decided he wanted to marry her. Obviously, Janet knows the protocol of courtship herself. She also knows how to bend it to her purposes. In Chapter VII, she told Beaumont that Madvig once kissed her in the same room in which she and Beaumont had talked the previous night—probably to let Beaumont know that he missed a chance to kiss her himself. His ignoring her hint spurs her into moving more boldly in Chapter VIII. Without telephoning beforehand, she comes to his apartment at nine o'clock in the morning to discuss Taylor's murder. Her visit is not merely investigative in intent. She has skipped breakfast so that she could have it with him, and, before leaving, she asks him to call her as soon as he learns anything, "no matter what time of day or night it is."

They agree, during breakfast, to turn up as much evidence as

135

possible in order to judge the truth of Madvig's confession. Madvig prevaricated about his role in the murder case before, and he may be doing it again. Only if they prove him guilty will Janet and Beaumont broach the matter of his punishment. Beaumont's search for evidence takes him to a speakeasy Shad O'Rory is known to frequent. The person he finds in the O'Rory camp, though, is Jeff Gardner. Beaumont acts very self-composed and nonchalant with the sadistic Jeff, even though Jeff beat him senseless less than a month before and has announced his intention of doing it again forthwith: Beaumont would rather take another beating than let Jeff know he's afraid. His coolness carries the day. Seizing his chance, he provokes a quarrel between Jeff and his chief, O'Rory, who has come in; as often happens in Hammett, it doesn't take much to set two crooks at each other's throats. Jeff kills O'Rory and leaves in the custody of the police, whom Beaumont had called in. By spotting and using his advantage, Beaumont removes two enemies while hardly lifting a finger.

Hammett introduces a scenic contrast next in order to invite a moral contrast, which he withholds. From the speakeasy where O'Rory dies, Beaumont goes to the stately home of Senator Henry. The last chapter restores the dignified Senator to the action, but only to name him his son's killer. Though no detective, Beaumont uses some neat detection to catch his man. Soon after entering the Henry estate, he tells both the Senator and Janet (who greeted him "with both hands out") that Madvig killed Taylor. His words gladden Janet because, spoken in her father's hearing, they let her out of her informal engagement to Madvig. The Senator's thoughts are elsewhere. Once Madvig knows he has lost Janet, he will have no reason to cover up for her father if arrested for Taylor's murder. Acting the bereaved, grief-racked father, Senator Henry plans to stop Madvig before he talks; a person who kills a son won't strain at killing a defected colleague. But Beaumont stops this alleged champion of due process from flouting due process; after he is prevented from killing Madvig, Senator Henry tries unsuccessfully to kill himself. He did well to yield to Beaumont on both counts. Naturally, the details of Taylor's death will force him out of the election. But even though he will lose his Senate seat, he'll escape sentencing: "His age and prominence and so on will help him," says Beaumont. "The chances are they'll convict him of manslaughter and then set the sentence aside or suspend it."

But Beaumont isn't done with the Henry family. Hearing that he's leaving town presently, Janet asks to go along. Weaving loose thematic threads, Hammett then shows Madvig coming to Beaumont's flat to ask his former aide to come back to work. That he frames his appeal with Janet in the next room brings in a nice irony: the woman Madvig loves is overhearing his conversation with the man *she* loves; what is more, her would-be lover is competing against her for the loyalty of her beloved. But no competition really exists. Besides turning Madvig down, Beaumont adds that Janet, who has walked into the room, is going to New York with him. Is his disclosure unnecessarily brutal? or an act of kindness in disguise? Though rattled, Madvig will soon brand Beaumont a traitor whom he wouldn't have wanted in his camp, anyway. By telling Madvig something he'd have learned for himself sooner or later, Beaumont is merely speeding the rejection. He may have also staged his farewell with Madvig to show Janet that he intends to start his life with her on the right footing; he won't be tempted to leave her in New York in order to return to Madvig. On the other hand, she can find little encouragement in Beaumont's last action in the book. While she looks at him, he is staring at the door which Madvig just used to make his exit. Does Beaumont miss him already? Does he regret giving him up for Janet?

II

Glass Key provokes many such questions. How long will Janet and Beaumont stay together? Does Beaumont have a job waiting for him in New York? One character mentions his New York background, but he shies away from the subject. His silence typifies the novel. We know very little about him and the others. For instance, nothing is said about Madvig's marriage to Opal's mother—the mother's name, how long she stayed with Madvig, or what happened to her. Hammett also never explains the Taylor Henry death as accidental or deliberate. These imponderables add to the novel's nonrepresentational effect. Hammett doesn't give us our bearings in *Glass Key*. Like *Red Harvest* before it, the work shows very little of the ordinary daily lives of everyday people. Often, a character's words will come out indistinct and be lost. The treatment of the scenes reflects the same sharp departure from naturalism or documentary realism. The book's first major development comes at the start of Chapter I, subchapter 4, with Beaumont's discovery of Taylor Henry's corpse in China Street. At the end

137

of the previous subchapter, Beaumont was leaving China Street, site of Madvig's casino. Only later does it become clear that he is returning to the casino after having been away, presumably to the race track. What never becomes clear to the characters are their purposes. Madvig wastes enormous effort pursuing a course of action, i.e., marrying Janet, that can never materialize. Furthermore, Hammett must have boosted his Marxist spirits a little by describing a free election—supposedly the safeguard and pride of a democracy—as both crooked and ineffectual.

Also expressive of the vexation posed by the tense, teeming city is the device of disjointing a character's words and body language from his meaning. The people in the book usually say more or less than what they mean; in addition to lying a great deal, they speak most idly when most deeply moved. This maneuver builds a mood of detachment, keeping us from identifying with them; you can't root for a stranger. It also deepens Hammett's portrait of the urban inferno; city dwellers, always on the watch for falling beams, can't live at full stretch. Madvig displays his heart and nearly loses everything because of it—his best friend, woman, daughter, and foothold in the city he has run for years. Rightly, Beaumont accuses him of mixing politics and sentiment; "I . . . think you've let yourself be outsmarted this time. First you let the Henrys wheedle you into backing the Senator. There was your chance to go in and finish an enemy who was cornered, but that enemy happened to have a daughter and social position."

Beaumont's words mesh with the grimness the novel sustains so well. While perhaps working on *Glass Key,* Hammett criticized Charles Francis Coe's now-forgotten novel about bootlegging and municipal corruption, *Hooch,* in terms that might have served as a warning to himself. He called *Hooch,* in 1929, "too trite and too formless to be good fiction, too stiff and too general and too thoroughly bowdlerized to be good reporting."[3] To free *Glass Key* of the flatness of journalism and the moralizing of much of the day's muckraking fiction, he described scenes of outstanding violence in clear, flat prose, and he built the played-down violence around a gallery of sinners. All the major figures in *Glass Key* commit a serious wrong, which usually involves betrayal. The betrayal spreads like cancer. Thompson believes that Madvig exploits Beaumont to further his personal and political interests.[4] Madvig is paid in full for his alleged sins. Janet and her father and O'Rory and Beaumont, his two

138

former proteges, all betray him. Even his daughter, Opal, throws in with his enemies, blaming him for Taylor's death without giving him a fair hearing.

Glass Key also gains unity of effect from careful selection. Though imposing no personal viewpoint or set of values, the book is full of hard edges and repressed anxieties; everybody is stiff, lonely, near the edge. Images of urban dislocation replace character analysis and moral statement; the de luxe living arrangements of Beaumont, Madvig, and the Henrys rest on a bedrock of vice and corruption. This grimness of tone and coloring might have influenced and even helped create the genre of *film noir* in the 1930s and 1940s. Films belonging to the genre, like the thrillers, *Street of Chance* (1942) and *Detour* (1946), usually treat loners who are also losers; though no loser, Beaumont suffers tremendously, and he lacks the strength of both the Op and Spade. The stark, bleak settings featured in *film noir* are often a function of darkness and rain; analogously, Beaumont finds Taylor on a dark, wet street the same day his horse wins a race run on rainy turf.

Sometimes, the grimness is overdone. Nolan calls *Glass Key* "a perplexing, frustrating book," adding, "We are never allowed inside any of the people . . . we see them all once-removed; we are forced to judge them strictly on what they say and do. Hammett never used the objective approach more stringently."[5] This approach includes showing the physical counterparts of emotions without revealing, let alone discussing, the emotions themselves. The technique of translating emotions and ideas to external behavior robs *Glass Key* of inner life. When the action calls for a telling insight, Hammett bathes it in melodramatic gleams. The book's dark glimmering surface reveals characters who resemble silhouettes or sheet-tin cutouts. The deadpan tragedy of *Falcon* has become a self-duplicating reflex, Hammett coasting in on the techniques developed in the earlier work. But these techniques don't suit Beaumont as well as they did Spade. He absorbs terrific punishment, and, in keeping with the book's starkness of line, twists his face into more expressions than a silent film actor (the book's historical relationship with the movies reaches both backward and forward) rather than explaining himself. And what a facial contortionist he is. He can make his eyes hard, cold, narrow, watchful, bright, or curious; they can also glitter, smolder, shine with malice, and shoot fire. Other melodramatic gestures include his shuddering, shivering, wincing, smoothing of his mustache, chewing his nails, or biting down on his cigars. Spade is a poker face by comparison. In the following passage, where he parades a typical array of over-done gestures, Beaumont acts more like a silent film hero than a literary character:

> Ned Beaumont's face, after a grimace of rage at the closed door, became heavily thoughtful. Lines came into his forehead. His dark eyes grew narrow and introspective. His lips puckered up under his mustache. Presently he put a finger to his mouth and bit its nail. He breathed regularly, but with more depth than usual.

A novel in which mannerisms and other forms of oblique discourse outrank direct statement of fact will invite a good deal of motive seeking. In *Glass Key,* the motives are often sexual. Kenney says that the friendship between Beaumont and Madvig is "so intense that it seems at time to approach the homoerotic." In concert, Bazelon calls Madvig "almost, indeed, a homosexual love-object" for Beaumont.[6] It is difficult to find evidence supporting this argument. Even Beaumont's final act of staring "fixedly" at the door Madvig has just exited from need have no basis in homosexuality. The sensitivity the two men show to Janet hardly befits homosexual love; there is no evidence that either is dangling Janet before the other to incite jealousy. Nor can an argument proving Madvig's homosexuality take root in his living with his mother; he also lives with his daughter. And what of Beaumont's living alone? This arrangement implies that, like his chief, he has no wife, but that, unlike him, he is a newcomer to the city whose roots lie elsewhere. Granted, he and Madvig are very close. But if Madvig hadn't prized Janet over him, he'd not have fired him for saying that she planned to drop him, Madvig, right after the election. Besides, the associations between Beaumont's name and the Renaissance—Francis Beaumont being a younger contemporary and perhaps collaborator of Shakespeare—suggest only the intense, exclusive sort of male friendship found in many literary works of the day, like *The Merchant of Venice* and *Julius Caesar.*

A much stronger case for homosexuality in *Glass Key* can be built around Jeff Gardner, Shad O'Rory's apish, bow-legged henchman. The scenes in which Jeff beats Beaumont are among the most sadistic and terrifying in hardboiled fiction, much of their brutality coming from the ogling, embracing, and sweet talking that accompanies the beatings. Jeff's hammering of Beaumont "becomes almost an act of

140

love,"7 says Kenney, and he is right. But it is love twisted into the form of hatred. Jeff's polite care and matey insistence that Beaumont, whom he calls his chum, enjoys being battered makes Jeff's battering of him repulsive: "I never seen a guy that liked being hit so much or that I enjoyed hitting so much," says Jeff before fetching Beaumont a haymaker that knocks him out for two hours. What rankles most about Jeff's words is their possible foothold in truth. Has this sadist found his partner in the masochism, parading as physical bravery, of Beaumont? Beaumont, whom Jeff calls a "massacrist," seems to invite Jeff's cruelty. At least twice, he goes out of his way to visit places where Jeff is in attendance. Jeff exudes menace. His powerful labor, as he chokes O'Rory, has a sexual rhythm. What is more, he seems to be performing this act of erotic cruelty for Beaumont's benefit:

> Grinning from ear to ear at Ned Beaumont, not looking at the man whose throat he held in his hands, Jeff began to take in and let out long slow breaths. His coat became lumpy over his shoulders and back and along his arms. Sweat appeared on his ugly dark face.

> *   *   *

> Grinning at Ned Beaumont, not looking at the man whose throat he held, Jeff spread his legs a little wider and arched his back. O'Rory's hand stopped beating the wall. There was a muffled crack, then, almost immediately, a sharper one. O'Rory did not writhe now. He sagged in Jeff's hands.

Nor is the sexual coloring of the slaughter lost on Beaumont: "Ned Beaumont was pale. He too was breathing heavily and moisture filmed his temples. He looked over Jeff's lumpy shoulder at O'Rory's face." He might have been watching a rape.

His fascination with Jeff's massive undulations could also point toward a universal statement. His apelike glower makes Jeff a throwback to an earlier evolutionary state, with which Beaumont has affinities (O'Neill's *Hairy Ape* [1922] and Raymond Chandler's *Farewell, My Lovely* [1940] are other works of the period that lean on the then-popular idea of post-Darwinian man). A different manifestation of Jeff's primitive force comes in his name. Just as a gardner protects green, growing things, so does Jeff's thick, raw sensuality merge

141

with the rhythms of the jungle, where he reigns as king (Jeff-Sp. *jefe,* or chief). But the violence this gardner sows poisons life as it sustains it. His evil compels us, because, like Beaumont, we recognize its vibrations in ourselves. The vision of depravity Jeff lends to *Glass Key,* Hammett's darkest novel, goes beyond capitalism and urban vice.

This primitivism gains strength from the many Freudian and Sophoclean motifs scattered throughout. Intergenerational sex comes in with the Paul Madvig-Janet Henry courtship and, more vividly, with the marriage of gray-haired, bespectacled Hal Mathews, a local newspaper publisher, and Eloise, who went to school with Opal Madvig. Other motifs refer to different aspects of Oedipal sex. Both Madvig's mother and Janet Henry's father have youthful eyes, implying hidden desires and drives. Perhaps Janet had these cravings in mind when she asked Opal, in her anonymous set of three questions, "Are you really too stupid to know that your father killed your lover?" Opal had good reason to ponder the question, since Madvig later claims to have killed Taylor with a cane, a phallic weapon, in their quarrel about sex. Another working out of the Laius complex, in which the father reverses the primary Oedipal drama by killing the threatening son, comes in Senator Henry's murder of Taylor. Janet's response to the unravelling of the murder, finally, echoes that of Antigone when she heard of her rebel-brother's death at the hands of Creon, king of Thebes. Janet turns angrily from her father, just as Antigone did from her father's brother, because he dishonored Taylor's body by leaving it where it fell. That Janet mentions her father's deserting Taylor's corpse twice shows that the desertion strikes her more deeply than the murder preceding it, which she talks less about. But the classic Oedipal revolt, in which the angry son strikes out at the father he wants to supplant, usually outshines the motif of the threatened, hostile authority figure. Thus several of the betrayals in *Glass Key* fit the pattern set by Oedipus at Phocis: Beaumont and O'Rory both turn on Madvig, their ex-mentor; in strangling O'Rory, Jeff kills *his* chief.

Commonly viewed as a phallic symbol, the key of the novel's title also calls up a Freudian reading. The glass substance of the key expresses the truth that, though powerful, sex also has a fragility that calls for delicate handling lest the key shatter. What Hammett's key refers to specifically is Janet's chances for happiness with Beaumont. Janet tells him about a dream she had with a glass key in it after

142

hearing his description of a recent dream of his own: "I was fishing . . . and I caught an enormous fish . . . and you said you wanted to look at it and you picked it up and threw it back in the water before I could stop you." The dream reveals opposing drives: though Janet has claimed enough of Beaumont's heart to get into his dreams, she also threatens his joy. Janet's answering dream—if it is a dream and not a fabrication—deals with some of the same themes, but more hopefully. In her dream, she and Beaumont find a house in a forest clearing. The house is full of food, which the hungry pair crave, but also full of snakes. They decide to try their luck. Under the doormat is a key which they use to open the door of the house. Then, having quickly climbed up to the roof, they watch the snakes slide into the forest. They then go into the house and eat the delicious food there. The feast makes Janet so happy that she woke up in laughter.

But she has more to say about her dream. After a week, during which she learns the facts of her brother's death, she admits having faked the ending. What really happened was that the key of glass shattered while unlocking the door, causing the snakes to rush out and crawl all over her and Beaumont. She woke up screaming from the dream, not laughing. Most of Hammett's critics have interpreted this dream pessimistically. "Apparently, the attempt to unlock the barriers which prevent fulfillment is to release vipers,"[8] says Parker. Reasoning similarly, Nolan and Edenbaum both share Parker's lack of confidence in the future happiness of Janet and Beaumont: "Hammett is telling us that they are in for a bad time, that they should not have fed their 'hunger,' for soon the snakes will overtake them,"[9] claims Nolan. Edenbaum explains how to avoid being overtaken by snakes: "The title of this novel . . . suggests once again the fear of unhedged emotion and thus of all human relationships. . . . The only safety is not letting down your guard in the first place: do without the food and you escape the snakes."[10] But Janet and Beaumont want to enjoy the food. And they have a decent chance. Certainly, the dangers facing them are less acute than those threatening Spade had he settled down with Brigid. Janet's outlook has darkened since she first talked about her dream; she also knows Beaumont better than she did. Perhaps, in her altered version of the dream's ending, she is denying the fiction that life contains enchanted cottages where babes in the woods can go for shelter and food. Beaumont is supposed to set store by this mature, realistic attitude. He is also meant to appreciate her knowledge that certain prizes are better ignored than won by force; the glass key breaks if jammed into the wrong lock or turned too sharply in the right one. Restraint, patience, and lightness of touch may help you enjoy the food without bringing on the snakes. But these virtues can be overdone. Somebody constantly on guard can't relax enough to reach for the food, let alone enjoy it. Life's banquets are savored by those who have hidden the fact, maybe even from themselves, that their guard is down. Perhaps included in Janet's new understanding of Beaumont is the importance of using indirection with him.

III

But who is this near-stranger for whom she gives up everything? Hammett called *Glass Key* his favorite among his novels because the clues "were nicely placed."[11] He might have added that he liked the novel so well because its hero resembled him so closely. The beginning of its first sentence, "Green dice rolled across the green table," prefigures the many gambles taken by the characters for the sake of fulfillment. But it refers as well to Beaumont, the novel's most compulsive gambler. Hammett also gambled a great deal. And, like Beaumont, he sported a mustache, dressed nattily, drank and smoked heavily, and had the flat chest indicative of a weak constitution. Then there are Beaumont's internal qualities. He has Spade's ability to gain the upper hand over people, even those who surpass him in money and power; as seen in his behavior with Jeff and O'Rory, he won't even give his victors the satisfaction of knowing they have defeated him. But what lies behind his facade of tough independence? Kenney says that "in Ned Beaumont . . . Hammett presents what may be his most interesting study in moral ambiguity."[12] Beaumont drips ambiguity, moral and otherwise. We can't call him a masochist, an opportunist, or a tough loner preserving his honor in a sleazy world because we don't know his reasons for acting. Like a Pirandello character, he wears his mask so well that it has become inseparable from his true self.

Can he separate his face, or true self, from the facade? He calls himself "a gambler and a politician's hanger on." Though he names Senator Henry Taylor's murderer, he is no detective. In fact, he hires a detective, Jack Rumsen, to do leg work for him in New York and to

144

later trace the machine on which Janet typed her incriminating, three-part messages. His neglect of the poor, the sick, and the jobless make him, along with his free spending, an unlikely Depression hero. Beaumont has sold out to the machine. A believer in the spoils system, he hands out bribes, sinecures, and patronage jobs in return for political favors. His ability to handle people makes him valuable to Madvig, especially in dealing with high-ranking officials like the D.A. or the chief of police. This ability comes forth in different ways. Affecting an elaborate casualness, he usually greets people he calls by name by saying "'Lo": " 'Lo, Walt," " 'Lo, Paul," " 'Lo, Lee." He can also be deadpan, ironical, charming, or melodramatic, as the situation demands. He is polite but firm with Senator Henry, whom he disarms and detains in the last chapter while calling him Sir. Other confrontations make him snarl. He lashes out cruelly at Janet, "I know whoever killed your brother did the world a favor." Nor does he spare Madvig's feelings when he tells his chief "in a low sure voice" that his political career is probably finished. He can speak out boldly because he stays informed. Every day, he reads a newspaper to keep up with the local developments he helped bring about. Evidently a voracious reader (like his creator), he remembers enough of the book of Judith in the *Apocrypha* to apply its lesson to Janet and her treachery toward Madvig. He will also leaven his bony intensity with good sense and moderation. When Opal agrees to help him find Taylor's killers if he promises to see them caught and punished, he answers, "I can't promise that. Nobody can."

His outstanding trait remains his intensity, perhaps because it clashes so vividly with the candor of his fair-haired, bulky chief. When asked about his long losing streak as a gambler, he answers, "I can stand anything I've got to stand." As has been seen, he backs up the claim by withstanding terrific poundings from Jeff. What is more, his facial contortions convey his keen sensitivity; his ability to take punishment (and enjoy it?) would mean less if his senses were dull. But he doesn't explain why he encourages Jeff to batter him. His lonely pride, his loyalty to Madvig, and the possibility of a masochistic streak have all been put forth as motives without being approved or ruled out. Perhaps we can know him better by seeing how he lives when he is not being battered. Drawn to old-world elegance (perhaps as a brake to the fast change booming around him), he enjoys the life style of a man of leisure. He smokes long, graceful cigars; he dresses

145

tastefully; when he doesn't walk, perhaps his favorite form of exercising, he travels around cities in taxicabs. He likes to start the day by having a white-jacketed waiter serve him breakfast in bed. The roomy, old-fashioned apartment where he dines so elegantly, with its high ceilings, fireplace, and red plush furnishings, defines him as a new-style racketeer. Again like Madvig, O'Rory, and even Senator Henry, he shows organized crime encroaching upon the class game; no simple roughneck, today's gangster, who already has money, affects gentlemanly airs to achieve social prominence. The main difference between Madvig and Senator Henry is that the Anglo-Saxon-named Senator has attained a station, symbolized by his daughter, that Madvig craves. What Beaumont craves can only be surmised. Perhaps Hammett made him grimace and shudder so much to hide his own puzzlement. His uniform practice of calling him by both names, Ned Beaumont (unlike both the Op, who is never named, and Spade who is usually referred to by his last name), reflects a tendency to romanticize rather than understand or convince.

Most of the novel's flaws stem from Beaumont. Edenbaum judges *Glass Key* "Hammett's least satisfactory novel"[13] because it ignores the motivation behind Beaumont's two most important acts—his allowing himself to be beaten rather than following through on his agreement to betray Madvig and his decision, at the end, to leave town with Janet Henry. Though Edenbaum's disclaimer overlooks Hammett's portrayal of both the bewilderment and insecurity of the American city, it does address the problem posed by a novel which bypasses a major element of novelistic art, i.e., motivation. The cool detachment that strengthened *Falcon* weakens *Glass Key* because it hardens into a manner used in place of sound plot construction: a few scowls and shudders from Beaumont, Hammett believes, will boost the plot more than a page of revealing dialogue or character analysis. *Glass Key* is a scamped, evasive novel, hardly deserving Julian Symons's praise as "the peak of Hammett's achievement."[14] Plausibility also deserted Hammett in his crafting of the book's key event, the murder of Taylor Henry. According to Janet, on the night he died Taylor ran after Madvig because Madvig's kissing his sister offended his sense of family honor. His moral outrage isn't credible. Not only was Taylor Opal's lover; he also brought other women to the apartment he had presumably rented for the private use of Opal and himself. Unfortunately, the two worst mistakes in *Glass Key* come in the most conspicuous spots—its main event and its leading character.

But these mistakes are redeemed in large part by many startling political and psychological insights, a complicated plot that stays on course despite the burdens imposed by serial publication, and a tonal unity that comes from Hammett's control of the off-key relationship between dramatic event and narrative voice; *Glass Key* can be characterized as a razor honed by the fumes and noises of the modern American city. Its sophistication and played-down intelligence will help it live longer than any other Hammett novel besides *Falcon*.

7

Season's Greetings

Perhaps because readers hope to find in *The Thin Man* (1934) a positive encompassing morality and come away disappointed, Hammett's last novel is also his most controversial. Some have even denied the artistic basis of the controversy; Parker, for instance, calls the novel "far and away Hammett's weakest effort."[1] Howard Haycraft's assessment is only a mite friendlier; though commending the novel for its humor, Haycraft judges it Hammett's "least typical and least important contribution."[2] The novel may have fared better in England. Perhaps anticipating disclaimers like those of the Americans Haycraft and Parker, Peter Quennell defended the work in his contemporary review. "It has every right to consideration on its literary merits,"[3] claims Quennell, whose fellow English critic, Julian Symons, echoed his praise nearly forty years later by calling the novel "a continually charming and sparkling performance."[4]

The book has many touches and trimmings indicative of Hammett's hand. As in all the other novels, it interrupts the action with a set piece (e.g., the Flitcraft story in *Falcon*) that illuminates the plot. It contains, in Dorothy Wynant, a debutante of twenty drawn to gangsters with the same force that compelled rich men's daughters in "The Gatewood Caper" and "$106,000 Blood Money." Dorothy also descends from Gabrielle Leggett Collinson in *Dain Curse,* another highly strung daughter of an eccentric inventor who fears that she's mad. But the novel resembling *Thin Man* most closely is the one standing closest to it in time, *Glass Key.* From *Key* comes the New York City setting, the physical cruelty, a title character who, with his mustache and tall, bony frame, looks like an aged, gaunt Ned Beaumont (or Dashiell Hammett), and the motif of hypergamy, or marrying above one's social class, as a symptom of social change: in Nora, Nick Charles, who may be the son of a Greek immigrant, has married the daughter of an industrial tycoon. (Another barrier that may come from *Glass Key* is that of age; in marrying Nora, who is fifteen years his junior, Nick follows a pattern formed by the newspaper publisher, Hal Mathews, Paul Madvig, and perhaps Beaumont.)

Contrasts between *Glass Key* and *Thin Man* clarify the later work as well as do comparisons. The sparkle and charm noted by Symons argue that Hammett followed his darkest novel with his lightest, most glittering one. Trim and mobile, *Thin Man* is both a murder mystery and a sophisticated comedy in the manner of a Philip Barry play; the New York holiday setting, witty repartee, and rich characters all invoke Barry's *Holiday.* Alvarez reads the work as more of a social critique than a detective novel: "The main interest is its view of New York just after the crash, with its nervy, slanderous parties, sporadically violent speakeasies, disintegrating boozing, and permanent hangovers."[5] It is easy to support this reading, the novel's steadiest presence being its aura of cosmopolitan glamor. The many phone calls to the Charleses' elegant hotel suite, the taxi rides through the humming city during Christmas week, and the hearty cheer with which the Charleses enjoy themselves all exude fun and bounce. The vacationing couple stay up till four or five o'clock in the morning. Interspersing bright conversation, they also eat Japanese food, go to a play, hear a private piano recital in Greenwich Village, and attend the opening of the Radio City Music Hall. While Nick is stalking a murderer or simply walking the celebrated Schnauzer, Asta, Nora will get her hair done, go to an art gallery, or shop at expensive stores like Saks or Lord and Taylor. The fun and festivity generated by this free spending put the Charleses at the center of New York City at its busiest, happiest season.

149

I

Thin Man opens on a casual note, expressive of its easygoing stylishness. While waiting in a speakeasy for Nora to finish her Christmas shopping, Nick Charles accidentally meets Dorothy Wynant, daughter of inventor Clyde Wynant. The forty-one-year-old Nick, who worked as a detective in New York before retiring to San Francisco to manage Nora's estate, asks to see Wynant, his former friend and client, whom he later describes thus: "Tall—over six feet—and one of the thinnest men I've ever seen. He must be about fifty now, and his hair was almost white when I knew him. Usually needs a haircut, ragged brindle mustache, bites his fingernails."

Nick will probably have to wait. Dorothy tells him that Wynant has been long divorced from her mother, Mimi, and that the family never hears from him directly any more. Nor has his absence affected their new life. Dorothy and her eighteen-year-old brother Gilbert live at the swank Courtland with their mother, who has married handsome, actorish Christian Jorgensen. Suddenly, it looks as if Nick will get to see Wynant sooner than expected. The inventor's lawyer, Herbert Macaulay, "a big curly-haired, rosy-checked, rather good-looking chap," says that he's in town. The next words Nick hears about him suggest that he may have brought trouble with him; Julia Wolf, his former secretary and mistress, has been found shot to death in her east side apartment. Thus the Jorgensen-Wynant cortege visit the Charleses the next day, Christmas 1932, but not to spread holiday cheer. Mimi Wynant Jorgensen, complaining that her money has run out, asks Nick to find her ex-husband. Despite her pious pleas, she is less worried about the welfare of her children than about keeping her younger husband in the nest. Nick resists being lured back into sleuthing. As well he might for safety's sake: the missing-person's case has spread to cover not merely murder but also the underworld; recent police investigations have linked Julia Wolf to gangster Shep Morelli. The novel is moving crisply and surely. By Chapter 6, it has brought in a family crisis, a murder, a group of suspects, an underworld figure, and a detective who won't detect.

The reluctant sleuth and the gangster meet presently. The next morning, Morelli appears in the Charleses' bedroom holding a revolver. He has come to say that he had nothing to do with Julia Wolf for the three months prior to her death. While protesting his innocence, he hears the police knocking at the door of the suite and asking to be let

150

in. He starts to panic. Hearing the sound of a key in the lock, he fires at Nick, whom he believes sent for the police. Nick has ideas of his own. Acting quickly if not graciously, he knocks Nora down and then throws a pillow at Morelli to foil his aim. A bullet creases his chest, anyway, causing a shallow wound along with some loss of blood. The tempo of the chapter demands that this wound doesn't faze him. His talk with the policeman who arrests Morelli both promotes suspense and steers the novel away from premature dramatic climaxes. These benefits both stem from Nick's presence of mind. No sooner is Nick congratulated on his great good luck at being saved than he points out that, by staying away, the policeman would have spared him from being shot in the first place. The intruding policeman has also hindered the investigation. First, his intrusion stopped Nick from finding out why Morelli wanted to tell him that he didn't kill Julia. Not eager to work with the police after their gaffe nearly killed him, he adds that he may not press charges against Morelli. In fact Nora offers Morelli a drink, undeterred by his shooting of her husband just minutes before. Even a police investigation of the near-murder of one of them can't shake the Charleses' poise or dim their bright style.

In front of others, that is; a graver mood takes hold at the Normandie suite after the police leave. Being shot has changed Nick's mind about ignoring the Wynant-Wolf case: "I've been pushed around too much. I've got to see about things," he says, with some of the resolve and purpose of a Spade or a Beaumont. Before he can take action, though, the novel shifts focus, Hammett wanting to add some human interest before bringing Nick into the case. Thus Dorothy arrives at the Normandie, her face bruised, cut, and scratched and her back striped with red welts. Her mother beat her to find out what she told Nick about her father's tie with Julia. Nick keeps edging closer to the case. Worried about Dorothy's safety, he allows the girl to stay with him and Nora. He also intends to go to Mimi's for dinner, where he and Nora have been invited, but where they are no longer expected because of his bullet wound. Nick wants some answers to the mysteries riddling the case. "We'll surprise them," he says, hoping that by catching Mimi off-guard he'll pry information from her that she wouldn't divulge otherwise.

Away from Nick, the case takes a new turn. A telegram sent from Philadelphia and signed Clyde Miller Wynant advises Nick to team with Herbert Macaulay, the Wynant family lawyer, to investigate the Julia Wolf murder. Still uncertain of what part, if any, he intends to play in the case, Nick sends the telegram by messenger to the Homicide Bureau of the city police before taking Nora to the Courtland. Julia Wolf's murder continues to mesh with the family drama burgeoning at the Courtland, Hammett keeping it an issue amid cocktails and chatter by having Gilbert introduce subjects like drugs, knife wounds, and criminal psychology. Conflict emerges when Nick says politely but firmly that Dorothy is at the Normandie, that he and Nora enjoy her company, and that she is welcome to stay as long as she likes. Undaunted by Mimi's growing irritation over having her wish that Dorothy be sent home ignored, he even adds vaguely, "She did say something about a beating." Nora, whose clever timing and judgment mean a great deal to the novel, quiets Mimi's rising wrath by creating a distraction, which she then claims might give Nick a relapse from his gunshot wound. The maneuver works. "The soul of politeness," Mimi sees her guests out and wishes them a good night.

But they don't relax for long. The next day brings big, slow, comforting John Guild[6] of the New York Police Department to the Normandie. Guild has with him a pistol that first came to the Charleses' suite in Dorothy's handbag. Nick had given the pistol to the police because he believed that it might have been used to shoot Julia. He was wrong. The jammed, rusted gun, with its broken firing pin, hasn't been fired for the past six months. Lieutenant Guild has other information to share: Wynant left town in October to work on an invention in private. To avoid being traced through his checking account, he empowered his lawyer, Macaulay, to convert his stocks and bonds into cash. Over the past three months, Macaulay has transferred $28,500 in converted shares to him through Julia. Guild also reports that Julia served six months in a Cleveland jail under a different name and that, until shortly before her death, she *had* been seeing Nick's assailant, Shep Morelli; the rackets keep intruding upon the case. Wynant keeps intruding, too, in a manner consistent with Nick's description of him as "a good guy, but screwy." In a letter he sends Macaulay from Philadelphia, Wynant complains that he only got $1000 of the $5000 the lawyer gave Julia a few days before she died. This news gets shoved aside by a new development. Within moments of learning of the thin man's motive for murder, Nick hears from Lt. Guild that Wynant has just tried to kill himself in Allentown, Pennsylvania.

The Wynant children come to the Normandie later that evening to await further report of their father. Young Gilbert, the crime buff,

152

student of Chinese, and aspiring author, continues to take both himself and his research seriously. His request for information about cannibalism prompts Nick to refer him to the story of one Alfred G. Packer in Duke's *Celebrated Criminal Cases of America* (a copy of which Casper Gutman once browsed in Spade's apartment). Packer's story both resembles and differs from other set pieces in Hammett—the dreams in *Red Harvest* and *Glass Key,* Leggett's Devil's Island letter in *Dain Curse,* and the Flitcraft episode in *Falcon.* Gilbert, who usually has a psychological theory for everything, doesn't understand the story: In the fall of 1873, Packer and nineteen other men set out from Salt Lake City to prospect for minerals. After weeks of hard weather, they chanced upon a friendly Indian chief who told them to go back to Salt Lake City. Ten of the prospectors disregarded his advice in favor of continuing their search for ore. Of these, six, led by Packer, dismissed the chief's warning to stay close to the Gunnison River. The following March, a wild-looking Packer appeared at an army outpost in Colorado, begging for food and shelter. By stages, it came out that Packer murdered and ate his five mates in order to keep from starving to death. He was later convicted of manslaughter and sentenced to forty years in prison, of which he served fifteen before receiving a pardon.

No wonder the story baffles and disappoints Gilbert, given his brittle erudition. But its relevance both to the *Thin Man* in particular and Hammett's thought in general isn't all that clear, either. Is it a veiled plea for social solidarity? Perhaps Hammett is warning us through Packer that the breakup of the social body leads to killing, dismemberment, and finally, cannibalism. What is more, we begin to enjoy the savagery we profess to hate once we take the first step of indulging it: "I had grown fond of human flesh, especially that portion around the breast," admits Packer. The survival of primitive drives in modern man carries forward from *Glass Key.* Thompson infers from the Packer story a reversion to the code of the jungle at the expense of the family:

> What we see in the Wynant-Jorgensen family, the Quinn family, the Edge family, and the Nunheim family is cannibalism masquerading behind the illusion of the family compact. In each case, the motivation for their vicious behavior is a combination of greed and a feeling of the necessity of self-survival, precisely the ingredients of the Packer story.[7]

153

But how do we block the tide of this savagery? Faced by starvation in the wilderness, all men will eat human flesh. And collective man is no better than the individual; five of the six members of Packer's party practice cannibalism. Any set of community values based on this savagery makes as little sense as one that ignores it. "It'd be swell if one of you people would make a clear and complete statement about something—it wouldn't matter what," grumbles Nick, referring to the jungle mentality ruling the others. If people act better in the mass than they do individually, Hammett doesn't argue the point in *Thin Man;* the police perform with uniform stupidity and brutality, and the motives governing Mimi's cruelty with her daughter don't improve when Mimi deals with others. Perhaps the Packer story contains the seeds of Hammett's farewell to fiction-writing. Following his lights, Hammett saw that he couldn't base a rational system like Marx's dialectical materialism on something as irrational and contrary as people. Even a program built on moral relativism can't banish cruelty and greed; moral relativism explains not only Packer's cannibalism but also the shoddiness that let Packer escape his captors for nine years and then set him free after serving but fifteen years in a forty-year jail term.

Before the chapter featuring Packer ends, it introduces another primitive strain—the code of vengeance. Mimi's handsome husband, Chris, fits the descripton of a scientist named Sidney Kelterman, who once accused Clyde Wynant of stealing his ideas when the men were experimenting in the lab. A letter sent to Jorgensen from Boston infers that he is not merely Sid Kelterman but a bigamist, as well. The writer of the letter, who signs herself, "Your true wife, Georgia," says she must see him. Her mention of money and her veiled threat to make trouble for him unless he sees her send Jorgensen-Kelterman to Boston at once, where he stays put for the rest of the novel. The Jorgensen-Kelterman sequence brings back the device, from "The Joke on Eloise Morey" (1923), of the biter-bit. Kelterman's plan to get back at Wynant by taking money Wynant gives Mimi goes amiss at the first whisper of vengeance from Boston.

Other out-of-town activity helps sharpen the plot, the would-be suicide in Allentown being identified as an unemployed carpenter and not Wynant. The Charleses take advantage of the reprieve to dine sumptuously and then attend a chic party in Greenwich Village, where Levi Oscant (i.e., Oscar Levant) gives a piano recital. After the music and the upper bohemian small talk, they still have enough energy to take Dorothy to the noisy, crowded Pigiron Club, a speakeasy both run and frequented by gangsters. Naturally, the debutante Dorothy is fascinated by the brutality of gunman Shep Morelli, who just got out of jail that day. Morelli tells Nick about the criminal girlhood and youth of Julia Wolf in Cleveland; no haven of integrity as in *The Great Gatsby,* Hammett's Midwest is as crime-ridden as his San Francisco, New York City, or Corkscrew, Arizona. Cleveland's Julia Wolf remains an issue. Back at the Courtland, Mimi produces a knife dangling from a broken key chain belonging to Wynant, which she claims to have found in Julia's apartment at the time of her death. Mimi says that the chain must have broken and slid away during the fight in which Wynant killed Julia. Yet Nick, normally cautious about making pronouncements, says that Wynant is innocent. (His adding, "I could have told you yesterday. I can't today," when asked to name the murderer, heightens narrative tension as the novel comes to an end.) Nick defies Mimi again when he invites Dorothy, who's afraid of being beaten again, back to the Normandie. Hitting, screaming, and kicking, Mimi needs to be kept away from Dorothy. The Charleses work together to protect the girl, Nora blocking Mimi's path to Dorothy and Nick wrestling Mimi to the sofa.

The next morning brings more trouble. Herbert Macaulay phones Nick to move their luncheon appointment up to breakfast. The lawyer wants Nick to help him arrest Wynant for killing Julia; he won't lie anymore to protect his guilty client. A Wynant does come to grief, but not the mysterious Clyde. Gilbert recently had a letter from his father, sending him to Julia's apartment and asking him to follow some instructions located between the pages of a book there. No sooner did he get to the apartment than he was jumped by a policeman and then beaten for resisting arrest. The subsequent failure of the police to turn up a copy of the book mentioned by Wynant makes Nick doubt that one ever found its way to Julia's apartment. "Maybe we ought to pay some attention to the things he [Wynant] hasn't pointed at, and the shop's one of them," Nick argues, after pointing out that none of the clues or leads materializing around Wynant has helped the investigation. Meanwhile, Mimi reports that her ex-husband has just left the Courtland, where he came to deliver some securities and a postdated $10,000 check for her and the children to live on during his upcoming absence. Naturally, Nick suspects that Wynant postdated the check to make sure that Mimi performed some service before getting paid. But Nick can't figure out the nature of the service, and Mimi needs only to stick to her story about Wynant's visit to pocket her money.

But she doesn't stick to her story. The ending of *Thin Man* follows the format of classic mystery fiction, Hammett bringing the characters together at the end for a demonstration of the evidence and the naming of the culprit. Mimi *was* being paid for a service, Nick reasons, but not a service to her ex-husband. Nick's sending the police to Wynant's shop, the only one of the inventor's haunts unmentioned in his communiques, discloses a body sawed into pieces and buried in lime along with some large clothes, a rubber-tipped cane, and a belt buckle bearing the initials DWQ. But these effects, not clues at all, were planted by the murderer to foil the investigation. The corpse buried in the shop didn't belong to any fat man with the initials of DWQ but to bony Clyde Wynant. The thin man's lawyer, Herbert Macaulay, killed him three months ago and then forged his signature on a letter giving him, Macaulay, power of attorney over the Wynant estate. The one weakness in his story, that he is the only person besides the murdered Julia Wolf to have seen Wynant alive in recent months, he shored up by paying Mimi to say that she spent time with him, too. Nick shows her the stupidity of backing Maculay's lie. Having already killed three people (besides Wynant and Julia, he murdered a police informer named Arthur Nunheim), Macaulay will kill Mimi, too, rather than risk having her change her story to the police about being with Wynant. What is more, the cash she got from Macaulay is a trifle compared to what she could realize as the mother and legal guardian of Wynant's children.

This well-judged appeal to her greed breaks the case. Outraged over being cheated, Mimi turns on Macaulay and exposes him. By relying on the lie of a liar, namely Mimi, the resolution of *Thin Man* observes probability; the key witness acting in character through to the end. The last chapter, which follows Macaulay's apprehension, maintains the same decorum. Because detection is no exact science, Nick details the steps in his reasoning for a skeptical Nora, whom he wants both to convince and impress. His chapter-long explanation gets much of its sting from the novel's first-person technique. Nick's parenthetical remarks, consisting of facts discovered later about the case, give the investigation a neatness that Nora can't find. Thus the parentheses both remove our doubts and preserve Nora's, protecting the life-giving tension between her and Nick. Hammett reconfirms the value of this tension in the book's last sentence: "That may be," Nora says in response to Nick's summation, "but it's all pretty unsatisfactory." She won't let Nick enjoy his achievement. In a hard, fighting world like ours, Hammett believes, we should distrust praise and prizes. They foster an unrealistic outlook that primes us for sorrow. Yet maturity of outlook also imposes limits. Though much of our behavior is goal-directed, very little of its rivets on problems caused by goal-attainment. Besides needing to be approached with caution, enjoyment precludes awareness; being concious of pleasure spoils pleasure because it shows us pleasure's ephemerality. Here is the link between Hammett and existentialism; here, too, may lie the reason for Hammett's popularity in France. We start scanning the sky for falling beams, and our good luck sours or disappears. Nick's elusiveness has kept Nora's love for him aglow. He pretends to hold back from her even while giving in. Better for their marriage that she remains a bit off balance than be too sure of him. Hammett agrees; though he mentions the watch and necklace the Charleses give each other for Christmas, he doesn't show the gifts being exchanged. All close relationships profit from the restraint his technique implies. Some of life's greatest rewards must be held back in order to spur incentive and thus extend limits. Hammett encourages this sort of growth. It would be good to know his opinion of the ending of the second Myrna Loy-William Powell *Thin Man* movie, *After the Thin Man* (1934), where Nora announces that she's pregnant. Though contrived and bogus-romantic, the announcement does fit his doctrine of means-oriented living.

II

Another benefit gained by the first-person technique is the mystery that builds around Clyde Miller Wynant. Nick's narration helps sustain the impression that the thin man is still alive; the device of making the missing person the leading suspect and then keeping him just out of view works better with one detective than with two, since a team of sleuths can cover more ground and block more avenues of escape. Hammett's treatment of Wynant tantalizes us. As the title character, scrawny Wynant is a presence throughout. The letters, telegram, phone call, suicide, and alleged meetings attributed to him with both

157

Mimi and Gilbert give his presence vitality. Hammett builds enormous reader interest by increasing both the number and intimacy of references to Wynant as the novel develops; from Philadelphia, Wynant comes to New York, where he supposedly phones and visits the other characters. The final stage in his emergence ironically shows him changing from murder suspect to murder victim at the end.

Other parts of the action work less well. Dorothy's wail, "I want to go home to Mamma," when she learns that Macaulay shot her father at the start of the last chapter, rings false, violating both the novel's portrayal of the Wynant family and the relationship of Dorothy and Mimi. Hammett sent Dorothy back to Mimi in order to leave Nora alone with Nick for their final confrontation. Dorothy hampers the narrative elsewhere, too. The pistol she claims to have been given in a speakeasy and which turns out a red herring causes more embarrassment than suspense. First, the inoperative pistol is introduced clumsily, as part of a long, elaborate story that has nothing to do with the main action. Next, Nick, with his sleuth's instinct, would have broken the pistol open to inspect its mechanism before turning it over to the police; even handling and looking at it should have told someone of his experience that the pistol hadn't been fired for months. Why clutter the novel with such an improbability? Creating plausible red herrings is a skill that sometimes deserts Hammett, as is shown later in his tedious account of the fortunes of the knife and chain found near Julia Wolf's corspe. The dull, flat prose in which the account is phrased conveys the strain Hammett underwent to keep the investigation moving:

> "Lieutenant Guild came to see me this morning . . . . First he showed me a piece of watch-chain with a knife attached to it . . . . Wynant could have given them to either of you, you could have stolen them or found them on the street or have given them to somebody who stole them or found them on the street, or you could have got them from somebody Wynant gave them to."

Brilliant in spots, *Thin Man* falters as an organic whole. It is hard to make sense of the novel's structure: the sophisticated comedy doesn't join hands with the murder case, and the undertones get lost in the wisecracks and cocktails. *Thin Man* undermines itself. Though its mode is comic, it suggests tragic depths. Unfortunately, to sound these depths is to destroy the novel's holiday glamor. The novel's leading ideas don't make our job any easier. Pointing to the numerous aliases adopted by the characters, Thompson cites "the problematic nature of identities in the novel":

> Jorgensen is discovered to be Kelterman; Julia Wolf is Rhoda Stewart, finally Nancy Kane; Albert Norman turns out to be Arthur Nunheim; and Sparrow is discovered to be Jim Brophy . . . . Ironically, almost all the action in the novel emanates from the assumption that Wynant is alive, an assumption that proves as misleading and hollow of truth as everything else.[8]

The large helping of sex served up in the novel, while introducing excitement, is usually rank. Nora's question about the Wynant-Jorgensen set, "Are they the first of a new race of monster?" could be answered by references to illicit sex: Mimi's mention of "my beautiful white body" and the erection Nick gets while wrestling her to the sofa in Chapter 25 lend erotic force to "those couple of afternoons we killed" he refers to in Chapter 6. But Mimi isn't the only one in the family with sexual designs on Nick. Both she and her son Gilbert believe Dorothy to be in love with him. Add to this maimed love triangle Gilbert's incestuous craving for Dorothy, the bigamy of Jorgensen-Kelterman, and Dorothy's claim that she needs a pistol to ward off her step-father's sexual advances, and Nick's estimate of the family, "They're all sex-crazy," makes good sense. (Gilbert, who asks Nick about incest, tells Dorothy that he's been seeing their father in order to win her attention, which he believes has been shunted to Nick.)

The problem of stable identities and the sexual tangle at the Courtland merge with Hammett's picture of family life, suggesting, says Thompson, "the almost total alienation of modern man."[9] Marriages crack all through *Thin Man*: Wynant and Mimi get divorced before the time of the book; Sid Kelterman walks out on two wives; the stockbroker, Harrison Quinn, wants to leave his wife for Dorothy; even the Charleses are celebrating Christmas away from home. Now the motifs of married sex and multinymity as functions of a shaky identity meet in the central chapter of this thirty-one-chapter work. They meet in the figures of little Arthur Nunheim, or Albert Norman, and the outsize woman he lives with, Miriam. The travesty of marriage Miriam and Nunheim (no home) have been enacting ends when a

159

police investigation breaks their domestic routine. Shaken by the presence of the police, Miriam throws a greasy frying pan at Nunheim before walking out on him. Then Nunheim slips away, to be murdered only hours later. Is Hammett saying, through this brief domestic sequence, what he said in the Packer story—that the collapse of the family brings on death? We can't say, because Nunheim-Norman is too minor a figure to carry a large share of the thematic load. Yet, by walking into the book in Chapter 16, he gets this load heaped on his back. He sags under it, never to reappear.

If Nunheim is too shadowy, the culprit, Macaulay, reflects even worse judgment and technique. "The murderer is the most weakly drawn character in the novel," complains Kenney, and Thompson agrees, calling Macaulay "the weakest villain Hammett ever created."[10] These judgments hit home. In fact, the title of the novel could refer to the insubstantial Macaulay, whose personality and role in the plot do lack force. Above all, he displays no traits that show him capable of sawing a friend's corpse to pieces; his being a poor shot with firearms denoting fear of, not attraction to, violence. Besides, Hammett doesn't give him a motive for murder, neither his law practice nor his home in fashionable Scarsdale appearing to need a fast infusion of Wynant dollars.

Hammett's treatment of Macaulay's guilt, as distinct from his character, shows skill and tact. After mentioning Macaulay on the first page, Hammett portrays him consistently as a man with something to hide. Every action that Macaulay engineers refers back to his guilt. To watch Hammett placing his clues is to watch a master of literary detection at his craft. First, we only have Macaulay's word for it that Wynant left New York in October to work on an invention; the only other person who has seen the thin man since his alleged departure, Julia Wolf, can't refute the story. Then, Macaulay protects himself by distracting the investigation. By spreading the falsehood that Julia pinched $4000 belonging to Wynant, he makes the police think she was killed for the money, none of which was found at her death-site. He continues to shunt suspicion away from himself by diverting the attention of the police. The story he makes up about an important message lying between some pages of a nonexistent book at Julia's, by wasting the time and energy of the police, cools the trail to himself. Some of his ruses he directs to Nick, whom he fears more than the police, having worked with him in the past. To quiet these fears, he plans to kill Nick. First, he makes Nick believe that the police

160

suspect him of murdering Julia and that Nick can relieve the pressure by apprehending Wynant, the real murderer. To banish any worries Nick may have about his own safety, Macaulay paints himself as a man of good will who has run out of patience. Refusing to protect Wynant, his treacherous client-friend, with any more stalls, he wants action. But the action he wants consists of luring an unsuspecting Nick to Scarsdale to be butchered.

Nick can handle Macaulay. Though retired six years from sleuthing, he has retained the sleuth's mentality and code of survival. Lacking the tough, knowing manner of Spade and the nervous intensity of Beaumont, he can carouse or work (his refusal of a drink in Chapter 27 proves that, though a hard drinker, he is no alcoholic). He also has the knack of defusing danger with wit. Waking up to the sight of Shep Morelli holding a pistol, he begins wisecracking immediately: "Do you mind putting the gun away?" he asks Morelli. "My wife doesn't care, but I'm pregnant." Wise-cracks make up a big part of his verbal strategy. Often, he will joke either to hide the truth that he is fencing hard with an interlocutor or to hold back facts. He holds back more than he tells. At different points he is told, "I never know when you're lying," "You're the damnedest evasive man," and "You'll never talk yourself into any trouble." He won't. He makes very few mistakes. Yet he can reply fully and accurately when he wants. Asked by Gilbert about the sensation caused by being stabbed, he explains what it feels like to be wounded by a knife *and* a bullet.

Like Agatha Christie's Hercule Poirot, he has a nose for lies, both their meaning and their cause. On the other hand, his suspiciousness hasn't jaded him. At times, his morality is more compassionate than legalistic. Righting wrongs and catching crooks must give way to deeper, more delicate needs at times. His respect for the feelings of Gilbert shows in his speedy rejection of Lt. Guild's suggestion that the boy lead the police to his father: "You can't ask that of him, Guild. It's his own father," says Nick protectively; betraying his father could haunt Gilbert for the rest of his life. This ripe heart knowledge typifies Nick. He knows he will miss life's richness by keeping his guard up all the time. Yet he can be whatever he has to be. He doesn't sacrifice logic for sentiment, and his tour of duty as a detective has honed his instinct for falling beams. He saved Macaulay's life when the two men fought together in the war; Macaulay showed his gratitude by getting Nick some jobs back in his sleuthing days. But Nick won't let this

161

background of mutual service or his liking of Macaulay, of whom he said in Chapter 2, "We had always gotten along nicely," stop him from arresting the lawyer. Hadn't the lawyer plotted to murder *him*?

III

In his farewell to literary detection, Hammett portrays the sleuth as a God figure; Nick saves Macaulay's life in the trenches and then takes it away after discovering the lawyer's guilt. Nor does he restrict his powers to crime-stopping. A brilliant talker, he controls conversations in which two subjects are being discussed at the same time and in which no speech answers the previous one. He pries things from Dorothy that she won't tell her family. He always comes back with a witty, tension-relieving answer to Nora's embarrassing questions. As has been said, he has taught her how the accidental and the oblique can bolster their marriage. Nora learns fast. Right after Dorothy starts talking about the psychological impact of childhood experience, Nick denies the importance of early influences. But without discounting other possibilities created by the subject; on the same page, Nora, alert to nuances, addresses him as "son," and minutes later, following her lead, Nick calls her "Mamma." The bond between them has been strengthened as smoothly as either could wish.

This bond needs all the help it can get to withstand the void threatening it. Perhaps Thompson is right to call *Thin Man* "a continuation and logical extension of the themes and concerns of the preceding novels."[11] Hammett's lightness of touch in his last book has not disguised his awareness of evil. Granted, the frolic and fun of *Thin Man* robs Hammett's career of a sense of artistic growth or deepening of vision. But other American writers of the century have also ended their careers on an artistic tailspin; Raymond Chandler's *Playback* (1958) and the late works of both Sinclair Lewis and John Dos Passos betray a weakening of intellectual fiber. The outlook put forth by *Thin Man* is less weak than it is modulated. Though kept on a tight rein, depravity stalks the novel. Nearly all the characters live for money and/or sex. The guests at the Courtland and Normandie, despite their fine manners and stylish clothes, reappear at the brawling speakeasy, the Pigiron Club. Furthermore, the emotions displayed in this gangster dive match those seen at the chic residences. The following description of Mimi as an enraged wildcat, as she fights off Nick in her suite, unleashes a ferocity that smashes all differences created by money and social rank:

> Mimi's face was becoming purple. Her eyes protruded, glassy, senseless, enormous. Saliva bubbled and hissed between clenched teeth with her breathing, and her red throat—her whole body—was a squirming mass of veins and muscles swollen until it seemed they must burst.

Hammett can be faulted for resisting the implications of this brilliant description. Though he saw lust, cruelty, and betrayal in Mimi Wynant and the others, he shied away from his vision. No demonic creator, he both shunned self-inquiry and refused to follow his inventiveness to its dark source after it abandoned Marxist writ. The sense of guilt and dread (Henry James's "black merciless things") that goads all creative artists dried his genius rather than feeding it. Though he calls attention to mysteries relating to matters of deep human concern, he never unveils them. The metaphysical issues called forth in *Falcon* and *Glass Key* and the ancient taboos grazed in *Thin Man* all get whipped into the froth of social comedy, where their terror fades. Hammett's primitivism survives chiefly as stylistic flourish.

This escapist way of dealing with his vision made fiction-writing more of a denial than a fulfillment for Dashiell Hammett. The Marxist implications of his stance must have made him smile thinly. He had reached an artistic dead-end. After *Thin Man,* he had nowhere either to grow into or to hide.

Notes

Chapter One

[1]Steven Marcus, "Dashing after Hammett," *City of San Francisco,* 4 November 1975, p. 18.

[2]Ralph Harper, *The World of the Thriller* (Cleveland: Case Western Reserve, 1969), p. 129.

[3]William F. Nolan, *Dashiell Hammett: A Casebook* (Santa Barbara: McNally & Loftin, 1969), p.121.

[4]Lillian Hellman, "Introduction," in Dashiell Hammett, *The Big Knockover: Selected Stories and Short Novels of Dashiell Hammett* (New York: Vintage, 1972), pp. xxii-xxiii.

[5]Marcus, p. 18.

[6]Joe Gores, "A Foggy Night," *City of San Francisco,* 4 November 1975, pp. 29-32.

[7]Hellman, p. ix.

[8]Steven Marcus, "Introduction," in Dashiell Hammett, *The Continental Op* (New York: Vintage, 1975), pp. xix-xx.

[9]Nolan, p. 54.

[10]John G. Cawelti, *Adventure, Mystery, and Romance* (Chicago: University of Chicago, 1976), p. 165.

[11]Vincent Starrett, "In Praise of Dashiell Hammett," *Books and Bipeds* (New York: Argus, 1947), p. 17.

[12]Dashiell Hammett, "From the Memoirs of a Private Detective," in *The Art of the Mystery Story,* ed. Howard Haycraft (New York: Grosset & Dunlap, 1946), pp. 418-19.

[13]William Patrick Kenney, "The Dashiell Hammett Tradition and the Modern Detective Novel," Diss., University of Michigan, 1964, p. 89.

[14]Walter Blair, "Dashiell Hammett: Themes and Techniques," in *Essays on American Literature in Honor of J.B. Hubbell,* ed. Clarence Gohdes (Durham, N.C.: Duke, 1967), p. 304.

[15]Dorothy Parker, "Oh Look, A Good Book!" *Constant Reader* (New York: Viking, 1970), p. 135.

[16]Dashiell Hammett, "Guessers and Deducers," *Saturday Review of Literature,* 16 April 1927, p. 734.

[17]George Grella, "Murder and the Mean Streets," *Contempora* (March 1970), p. 8; Raymond Chandler, "The Simple Art of Murder," in Haycraft, ed., p. 235; Joe Gores, *Hammett* (New York: Ballantine, 1976), p. 254; Ross Macdonald, "The Writer as Detective Hero," in *The Mystery Writer's Art,* ed. Francis M. Nevins, Jr. (Bowling Green, Ohio: Bowling Green Popular Press, c. 1971), p. 300; in Blair, p. 303.

[18]Ernest Borneman, "Black Mask," *Go* (February-March 1952), p. 66.

[19]Ross Macdonald, "Homage to Dashiell Hammett," *Mystery Writers' Annual* (1964), p. 8; David T. Bazelon, "Dashiell Hammett's 'Private Eye,' " in *The Scene Before You: A New Approach to American Culture,* ed. Chandler Brossard (New York: Rinehart, 1955), p. 181; A. Alvarez, "The Novels of Dashiell Hammett," *Beyond All This Fiddle* (New York: Random House, c. 1969), p. 210.

[20]Gores, *Hammett,* p. 8.

[21]Nolan, p. 2.

[22]Leonard Moss, "Hammett's Heroic Operative," *New Republic,* 8 January 1966, p. 33.

[23]Cawelti, p. 165.

[24]Marcus, "Introduction," p. xviii.

[25]Cawelti, pp. 163-64.

[26]Frederick H. Gardner, "Return of the Continental Op," *Nation,* 31 October 1966, p. 456.

[27]Dashiell Hammett, "Introduction," *Creeps by Night: Chills and Thrills Selected by Dashiell Hammett* (New York: John Day, c. 1931), pp. 8-9.

[28]In Donald Ogden Stewart, ed., *Fighting Words* (New York: Harcourt, Brace, c. 1940), p. 54.

[29]Ellery Queen, "A Letter from Ellery Queen," in Dashiell Hammett, *The Creeping Siamese* (New York: Dell, 1950), p. 7.

[30]Alvarez, p. 209.

[31]Macdonald, "Homage," p. 8.

[32]Alvarez, pp. 211-12.

[33]"The New Books," *SRL,* 11 June 1927, p. 901; "The New Books," *SRL,* 9 February 1929, p. 670.

[34]Kenney, pp. 86-87.

[35]George J. Thompson, "The Problem of Moral Vision in Dashiell Hammett's Detective Novels," Diss., University of Connecticut, 1971, pp. 179-80.

Chapter Two

[1]Erle Stanley Gardner, "The Case of the Early Beginning," in Haycraft, ed., pp. 206-7.

[2]Chris Steinbrunner and Otto Penzler, eds., *Encyclopedia of Mystery and Detection* (New York: McGraw-Hill, c. 1976), p. 105.

[3]Nolan, p. 27.

[4]William Ruehlmann, *Saint with a Gun: The Unlawful American Private Eye* (New York: New York University, 1974), p. 64.

[5]Frederick Jackson Turner, *The Frontier in American History* (New York: Holt, 1920), p. 37.

[6]Nolan, pp. 53-4.

7Chandler, p. 237.

8Nolan, pp. 23-4.

9Arguing from internal evidence, Ellery Queen dates the composition of "A Man Named Thin" in "the mid-1920s": "Introduction," in Dashiell Hammett, *A Man Named Thin* (New York: Ferman [Mercury Mystery No. 233], 1962), p. 13.

10Nolan, p. 39.

11*Ibid.,* p. 43.

12Marcus, "Introduction," p. xxiii.

13*Ibid.,* pp. xxiii-iv.

14Philip Durham, "The Black Mask School," in Nevins, ed., p. 216.

15*Ibid.,* p. 209.

16Joseph Blotner, *Faulkner, A Biography* (New York: Random House, c. 1974), p. 741.

Chapter Three

1Gores, Hammett, p. 111.

2Thompson, p. 7.

3*Ibid.,* pp. 36-7.

4Cawelti, pp. 171-2.

5Thompson, pp. 38-9.

6André Gide, "An Imaginary Interview," trans., Malcolm Cowley, *New Republic,* 7 February 1944, p. 186.

7Robert B. Parker, "The Violent Hero, Wilderness Heritage and Urban Reality," Diss., Boston University, 1971, p. 95.

8Jon Tuska, *The Detective in Hollywood* (Garden City, N.Y.: Doubleday, 1978), p. 159.

9Thompson, pp. 20-1.

10Kenney, p. 103; Tuska, p. 168.

11Ruehlmann, p. 71.

Chapter Four

1E.H. Mundell, *A List of the Original Appearances of Dashiell Hammett's Magazine Work* (Kent, Ohio: Kent State University Press, c. 1968), p. 25.

2Thompson, p. 71.

3Alvarez, p. 208.

4Kenney, pp. 103-4.

5Thompson, p. 56.

Chapter Five

1Robert I. Edenbaum, "The Poetics of the Private Eye: The Novels of Dashiell Hammett," in Nevins, ed., p. 99.

166

²Thompson, p. 121.

³Macdonald, pp. 8, 24.

⁴Marcus, "Introduction," p. xii.

⁵In Nolan, p. 61.

⁶Thompson, p. 117.

⁷Edenbaum, p. 100.

⁸Dashiell Hammett, "Introduction," *The Maltese Falcon* (New York: Modern Library, 1934), pp. viii-ix.

⁹Ruehlmann, p. 5.

¹⁰See Note 3, above.

¹¹Macdonald, p. 8.

¹²Moss, pp. 32-3.

¹³Kenney, p. 108.

Chapter Six

¹J.B. Priestley, "A Close-Up of Chandler," *New Statesman and Nation,* 16 March 1962, p. 379.

²Gores, *Hammett,* p. 185.

³"The New Books," *Saturday Review of Literature,* 27 April 1929, p. 961.

⁴Thompson, p. 135.

⁵Nolan, p. 69.

⁶Kenney, p. 86; Bazelon, p. 188.

⁷Kenney, p. 93.

⁸Parker, pp. 117-18.

⁹Nolan, p. 72.

¹⁰Edenbaum, pp. 118-19.

¹¹Reported in Elizabeth Sanderson, "Ex-Detective Hammett," *Bookman,* 74 (January-February 1932), 518.

¹²Kenney, p. 94.

¹³Edenbaum, p. 117.

¹⁴Julian Symons, *Mortal Consequences* (New York: Harper & Row, c. 1972), p. 139.

Chapter Seven

¹Parker, p. 118.

²Howard Haycraft, *Murder for Pleasure: The Life and Times of the Detective Story* (1941; rpt., Biblo and Tannen, New York: 1974), p. 171.

³Peter Quennell, "Books," *New Statesman and Nation,* 26 May 1934, p. 78.

⁴Symons, p. 140.

[5]Alvarez, p. 210.

[6]By contrast, the John Guild of the original, unfinished version of *Thin Man* was thin, nervous, and intense; see *City of San Francisco,* 4 November 1975, pp. 32Aff.

[7]Thompson, p. 182.

[8]*Ibid.,* pp. 187-88.

[9]*Ibid.,* p. 170.

[10]Kenney, p. 106; Thompson, p. 170.

[11]*Ibid.,* p. 169.